WHO RULES EL PASO?

PRIVATE GAIN, PUBLIC POLICY,
AND THE COMMUNITY INTEREST

WHO RULES

EL PASO?

by
Carmen E. Rodríguez
Kathleen Staudt
Oscar J. Martínez
Rosemary Neill

CFC
COMMUNITY FIRST COALITION

Community First Coalition
P.O. Box 12681
El Paso, Texas 79913
facebook.com/cfc915/
http://communityfirstcoalition.org
communityfirst915@gmail.com

Community First Coalition Constituent Organizations:
American Library Association—El Paso Chapter; Border Network for Human Rights; Border Regional Library Association; Chicano History Project; El Chuqueño; Hope Border Institute; Lincoln Center; LULAC Council 132; Main Library Friends; Mexican American Cultural Institute; Paso del Sur; Raza Organize; Reforma Library Organization; Social Justice Education Project; Texas Library Association—El Paso Chapter; Sancturary4LongevityProject; Union for Development and Quality of Life; UTEP Retired Professors; Velo Paso Bicycle-Pedestrian Coalition; Wise Latina International.

FIRST EDITION

ISBN: 9781710689044

Printed by Kindle Direct Publishing, an Amazon.com Company
Available in print and Kindle format from Amazon.com

Book design & typesetting by Vicki Trego Hill,
Trego-Hill Publications, El Paso, Texas.
Cover design by Mona Pennypacker,
Acorn Creative Studios, El Paso, Texas.

Acknowledgments

Many thanks to the following individuals for their ideas, suggestions, and direct contributions to this booklet, including providing editing assistance, research data, anecdotal evidence, and descriptive text that has been incorporated into several of the sections: Marilyn Guida, Marshall Carter-Tripp, Katherine Brennand, Verónica Frescas, Loida García Febo, Virginia Martínez, Monique le Conge Ziesenhenne, Sito Negrón, Margaret Neill, Sharon Amastate, Oscar Baeza, Carol Brey, Jackie Dean, Yolanda Leyva, PhD, Marsha Labodda, Gretchen Trominski, Vona Van Cleef, Judy Ackerman, Sharon Miles-Bonart, PhD, Rick Bonart, DVM, Janaé Reneaud Field, and Richard Teschner, PhD.

Contents

Introduction

THE COLLECTIVE

To answer the question, "Who rules El Paso," a reader might respond that the mayor and city council representatives rule the city of El Paso. On deeper examination, less visible forces appear to shape representatives' decisions. Of course, every city has influential and powerful people who try to sway and lobby elected officials on certain issues important to them. We believe, however, that much more than that goes on in El Paso and worse, that it is largely accepted. As many in the know will say, that's just the way things are done here.

Recently, those of us who closely follow developments at city hall have become aware of the degree to which non-elected, multimillionaires and billionaires have consolidated their influence to control important economic/financial policies, decisions and outcomes customarily within city council's purview. El Paso is no different from many other cities in the United States where, since the 1970s, those at the top of the economic hierarchy have significantly increased their wealth as a result of the restructuring of the economy and the implementation of conservative government policies (tax cuts for the rich, deregulation, etc.) that disproportionately have favored the well-to-do. As the wealth of local magnates has increased, so has their power over local affairs. The opposite is true of the middle class and working people, whose income has seriously stagnated and whose influence over local policies has greatly diminished.

Technology and open government requirements have helped us to discover, understand, discuss, and share our findings about the situation in El Paso among our Community First Coalition members. However, we realized the entire voter population should have access to this information in one condensed source, and thus our decision to publish a book.

Interestingly, the group of individuals who currently comprise the "powers that be" that we frequently reference in this book are a relatively new economic force in our region. This crop of movers and shakers are not members of the old El Paso families that historically controlled the local economy. In fact, in a month-long series published in the *El Paso Times* in June 1991, just one of the individuals we identify in this book is mentioned (briefly). The articles analyzed our city's power structure at the time. Significantly, in an article that focused on the leaders who "get things done," ten individuals, including three well-connected elected officials, two developers, two bankers, one attorney, one business owner, and one educator are mentioned—and all were of European American extraction. Another article described two organizations, EPISO (El Paso Interreligious Sponsoring Organization) and the local chapters of the national organization LULAC (League of United Latin American Citizens), as being effective in demanding attention for Hispanic needs. Also mentioned were the rising binational industrialists from Ciudad Juárez who were involved in the assembly industries that relied on low-cost labor in Mexico at export-processing factories. Two other articles entitled, "Women, Hispanics, Blacks Invading Power Structure" and "Hispanics Shove Way into Power," focused on the growing diversity among newcomers including El Concilio de El Paso, an umbrella organization of approximately thirty organizations. In the last article, "Power: Who runs El Paso?," the top five powerholders were identified, including two Spanish-surnamed people, Alicia Chacón and Hector Holguin, and the "king of power," Jonathan Rogers, "a banker-turned-mayor turned banker." As another article in this book documents, various descendants of Rogers contributed enough funds to the current Mayor Dee Margo to make the top-twenty list. Many of the people highlighted in the near-thirty-year-old 1991 article have either died or moved away.

The case studies in this publication are issues that many El Pasoans have heard about in the local news media, but they are covered in greater detail in this book, which includes sources and citations. We endeavored to make the connections and draw the conclusions that are often left out of newspaper and television news reports. We put the spotlight on downtown boondoggles past and planned—all within the impending disaster of a heavily indebted city and citizens burdened with high property taxes. Our hope is that this information will contribute towards a better-informed, more engaged voting public so that we can begin the process of re-installing a democratic and more representative city government.

Recent Developments and Public Concerns

In the sphere of local public-decision making, numerous actions recently taken by city leaders represent the wishes of wealthy people and special interests far more than they represent the public will. This pattern resembles what happens in Washington, D.C., where corporations and billionaires dictate the national agenda. The system in place in El Paso caters to developers and other business elites, while, with some exceptions, city representatives show little regard for what the citizenry thinks. To put it mildly, taxpayers have become weary of the way the city spends the people's money.

Two highly unpopular, tax-supported projects undertaken by the city largely on behalf of economic elites can be cited as a major source of the perception that most of the city's leaders discard public opinion regarding expenditures. One is the controversial baseball park approved by the city in 2012 essentially to serve the interests of the MountainStar Sports Group (see Section II). The other is the thus-far frustrated effort to build an arena in Duranguito that would hold sporting events desired by the MountainStar Sports Group and its supporters (see Section I). Other actions by city leaders that have eroded the public trust include:

- The building of an unneeded, expensive streetcar system that is used by very few people.
- The swap of 2,300 acres of publicly owned land in the city's northeast for forty-four acres of land adjacent to Interstate-10 on the west side owned by billionaire Paul Foster (see Section VII).
- Payment of highly inflated prices for private properties in Duranguito to secure the area for the building of the controversial arena (see Section I).
- The plan to squeeze the proposed Mexican American Cultural Center into the historic downtown library, a move that would yield a second-rate center while taking away 40 percent of the library's space (see Section VI).
- Intractable city opposition to a 2018 popular citizen ballot proposition to save the Lost Dog Trail from development. Yet the people defied the city, with almost 90 percent of the voters approving the initiative (see Section VII).

In 2020, El Pasoans are particularly troubled by the city's growing public debt, rising property taxes, land deals that favor developers, and a political system that is excessively influenced by campaign contributions, which gives the advantage to candidates who receive large donations from wealthy patrons (see Sections III and IV). Too many of our leaders and bureaucrats, as well as some magnates, are out of touch with the community, and the citizenry must act to bring about much needed change.

Who Wields Power?

Officially El Paso is a democratic city where citizens choose their leaders and, theoretically, those who govern carry out the public will. In reality, El Paso is like many other cities in the way that money largely determines who gets elected to office and who has the advantage in influencing decisions made by city leaders. With rare exceptions, coalitions made up of city leaders and business interests determine the way that growth and development take place. Economic elites who contribute to political campaigns inevitably acquire an inordinate amount of influence in public decision making once their candidates make it to office. This is not to say that elected officials automatically follow the instructions of those who fund their campaigns, but it is to say that donors, especially big donors, have much greater access to officials and much greater influence over public decisions than ordinary folk. As the saying goes, "money talks."

In El Paso, perhaps half a dozen wealthy individuals wield disproportionate power and influence over local affairs. It is well known that developers/businesspeople Paul Foster and Woody Hunt are at the top of that exclusive pyramid. Both are recognized for their positive contributions to the local economy and for their philanthropy, but at the same time many El Pasoans are uncomfortable with the way they have shaped decision-making at city hall to their benefit and to the detriment of taxpayers. The baseball park and the proposed Duranguito arena exemplify that influence (see Sections I and II).

Foster and Hunt have also been criticized for their role in the selection of Dr. Heather Wilson as president of UTEP (in 2019). Ex-congressperson and business-friendly Wilson is not a professional educator, and she clearly lacks the academic and personal qualifications to lead a large border university. Her anti-LGBTQ voting record and weak support for students of color clearly made her a controversial choice (see Section V). Further, considering the recent massacre at a local Walmart store by a white supremacist who was armed with an assault weapon, is it acceptable for UTEP to have a president who has an A rating from the National Rifle Association (NRA)? Presumably she approves of the easy availability of firearms. Is that good for UTEP students, professors, and staff?

Other examples can be cited of the excessive leverage exercised over the city by wealthy individuals. Citizens need to be well informed to counteract initiatives that go against the public will. In many ways, 2020, an election year, has become a watershed year for the pushback from El Pasoans about the budget, controversial projects, and the way decisions appear to be made without regard for public input. We applaud these valiant and courageous efforts.

About the Title

The title of this publication was inspired by the famous work of sociologist William Domhoff, Professor Emeritus at the University of California Santa Cruz, who fifty years ago wrote *Who Rules America?*, now in its seventh edition. As Domhoff strikingly said, "the idea that a relatively fixed group of privileged people might shape the economy and government for their own benefit goes against the American grain." While Domhoff's books focus on the national level, his concepts and methods can be applied to local levels, as other sociologists and political scientists have done.[1] Domhoff asks three questions about power: Who benefits? Who governs? Who wins? We do not and cannot comprehensively cover all these questions in this short book. However, we make a start in this, the first of what could be a series focused on our city's weak democratic institutions.

I. The Fight for Duranguito— and Against Taxpayer Abuse & Deception

CARMEN E. RODRÍGUEZ[1]

A dispute has been looming since 2004 over downtown revitalization and the proposed eradication of old Mexican American neighborhoods, notably South El Paso and Duranguito. The dispute has been riddled with concerns over the excessive influence of private interests in city projects, the proposed use of eminent domain, gentrification, hostility over historic preservation, city government neglect and indifference, including the displacement of low-income immigrants, among others. The manner in which this ambitious endeavor was initiated and propelled by "the powers that be,"[2] against the will of the residents, their supporters, historic preservationists and social justice activists created divisiveness and strife in the community.

This story relies heavily on timelines created and posted by Paso del Sur, a grassroots organization created to counter the destruction of the barrios. It is also based on the writer's personal knowledge and experiences. There is much more to this story than can be covered here. This is simply a brief sketch of some of the events, the people and the struggles that have transpired from 2004 to 2020.

Barrio or Blight?

Local magnates who conceived the downtown revitalization plan knew that the real estate adjacent to downtown border crossings had enormous economic potential. They envisioned future big box stores, sports stadiums, and other amenities for residents and visitors. Since the tycoons' view of the barrios was from a distance, literally and figuratively, they saw mostly neglect and blight: old, dilapidated buildings, overcrowding, and misfortune. Up close, however, the view was one of struggling yet thriving neighborhoods offering affordable housing, pedestrian-friendly living, accessibility to jobs and services, architecture from bygone eras, and the warmth and familiarity of culture and language.

For more than one hundred years, immigrants and workers who crossed the border saw that in order to achieve the American Dream for themselves and their children, they had to move their families to the only place that made sense considering their economic means. The barrios (neighborhoods) have made it possible for many generations of Mexican American families to transition, adapt, prosper then move on to improved conditions, thus making room for newer Americans. The traits are common to most barrios but especially so to El Paso's oldest barrios, Duranguito, Chihuahuita, and El Segundo. Those who see only blight have characterized support for the barrios as "glorifying poverty." But barrio supporters see it differently; they have been ardent critics of the city's neglect of these areas and have been strong advocates for improving housing conditions in the barrios.

A Secret Group with a Secret Plan

Starting in 2004, the community began to hear rumblings of a secret organization, the Paso del Norte Group (PDNG), comprised of prominent millionaires from both sides of the border who were working on a regional revitalization plan. The founder was Bill Sanders, a former El Pasoan who had returned a reputed billionaire, known internationally in real estate development circles after making his fortune in Chicago creating and investing in Real Estate Investment Trusts (REIT).[3] Connecting with the likes of magnates Woody Hunt, Paul Foster, Alejandra de la Vega Foster, and Sergio Bermúdez, the PDNG quietly recruited more than 350 prominent business and civic leaders and assembled a powerful and influential band of movers and shakers. Their apparent mission: to change the landscape and the look of downtown and bring grand scale economic development to the border, as well as increased prosperity to future investors.

The secret plan called for the acquisition of large tracts of land on both sides of the border through the use of eminent domain, if necessary. Naturally, residents of the areas targeted were concerned and disturbed that a powerful group of the super wealthy was making secret plans about their homes and neighborhoods.

Mayor Wardy: "The Experts Know What They Are Doing"

In early 2005, the public began to learn more details about the PDNG effort. At a city council meeting on February 15, 2005, it became clear the city was ready to form a public-private partnership with PDNG. During the meeting, Mayor Joe Wardy quelled concerns about lack of consultation with residents and neighborhoods and urged quick approval, stating the experts knew what they were doing. A majority of five council members voted to approve the partnership.[4] Claims of conflict of interest against members of city council who were also members of the PDNG were suppressed with assurances that no one would profit from the plan.[5]

When the official plan was publicly unveiled at a special city council meeting held at the Plaza Theatre on March 31, 2006, the controversy quickly unfolded. Plan proponents and would-be investors applauded and cheered; community activists, who were marching nearby in celebration of Cesar Chavez Day, chanted, *"El Barrio No*

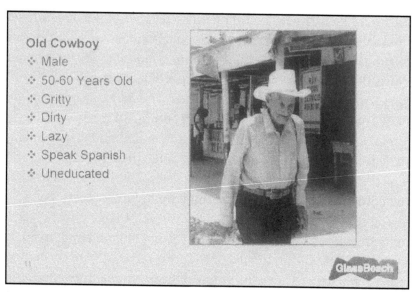

Image of downtown, according to Glass Beach.

Se Vende," (The barrio is not for sale), vowing to fight the plan and protect the barrios. The Catholic Diocese of El Paso understood the plan's ramifications and in an eloquent appeal in the form of an open letter to city council, Bishop Armando Ochoa called the plan unjust and divisive and warned against disregarding and displacing the poor and diminishing low-cost housing.[6]

A Revitalized Downtown Would Attract "Beautiful People"

One of the first steps (or missteps) taken by the partnership to advance the plan was the hiring of a branding firm, Glass Beach of San Francisco,[7] to renew El Paso's image. The firm's presentation to the city on July 19, 2006, included slides depicting the perceived present image of El Paso and the expected future image after renovation.[8] In one fell swoop, or rather, two slides, this branding firm not only failed to impress and inspire, it insulted the Hispanic community with glaringly racist and elitist imagery. This angered social justice

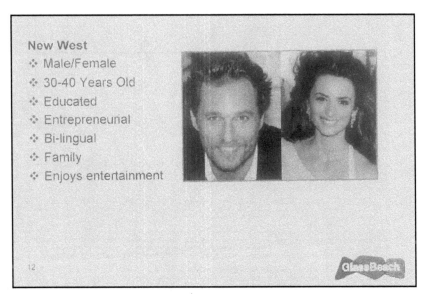

Image of downtown after renovation, according to Glass Beach.

activists and offended many Mexican Americans not connected with PDNG. Most outrageous of all, our city representatives failed to speak up for our community and instead endorsed the $150,000 Glass Beach Study!

The leadership of PDNG[9] assigned City Manager Joyce Wilson, who also happened to be a member, to take the reins of city forces and direct public resources to achieve city approval of the plan.[10] The city council, on October 31, 2006, officially adopted the PDNG's plan (prepared by SMWM Future Urban Planning Design, also of San Francisco), which became known as the Downtown 2015 Plan. The plan was described in glowing terms, promising El Pasoans a glorious future.[11]

The Opposition Organizes and Proponents Prepare to Prosper

The opposition group Paso del Sur, organized under the leadership of historians and activists Dr. David Romo and Dr. Yolanda Leyva,

5

Wilson, Joyce A.

From:	Wilson, Joyce A.
Sent:	Wednesday, April 19, 2006 7:21 AM
To:	'mdeckert@pasodelnortegroup.org'
Cc:	Adauto, Patricia D.; Hamlyn, Deborah G.; Lozano, Juliet; Firth, Sylvia B.
Subject:	PDN/Downtown Plan Process
Importance:	High

Myrna:

[1] Per our discussion last Friday, here is a preliminary outline of those things I believe are critical to advancing the PDN Downtown Plan to the formal City Plan Commission/City Council plan amendment process. Without these items being addressed effectively, I believe it will be difficult to get this plan through the formal public process for approval without substantial changes and dilution of the purpose/intent.

[2] I am rushing to get this to you this a.m. for your committee meeting, and have not had a chance to have Pat and/or Debbie comment and edit as they deem appropriate. Therefore we may be sending you an additional update later in the week. For now, these are the essential elements that need attention.

[3] (1) This needs to become a City/PDN process - so there is a clearer partnership. Right now it is being driven by PDN and we are running behind it. Also, there need to be more voices in the community information/education process - as it is primarily a Bill Saunders/Myrna Deckert team - and I am concerned that folks will start focusing on individuals not the organization as the driver of the plan/changes. Need to enlarge the group/face of PDN for purposes of this plan.

[4] (2) Communications. This is a clear weakness right now, as I discussed nearly two weeks ago. I've loaned our PIO for the short term to help you get this group organized and focused on a proactive messaging and information/public relations strategy. This is critical. You need to have resources devoted solely to this area for the next 60-90 days doing the following:

> [5.8] – Convention Center/Arena. I'd downplay this as a longer term issue as it is probably the lightning rod for tax increases for folks. Need to have a coordinated analysis of this v. current convention center with a hotel needs assessment (which City is doing) for downtown. This will give us the strategy to figure out the public/private partnership for this aspect of the plan.

Joyce Wilson issues instructions to city staff including the city attorney.
Inset—*Reference by Wilson that arena is "the lightning rod for tax increases" and should be downplayed.*

initiated a formidable grassroots resistance movement. Segundo Barrio resident and community leader Guadalupe Ochoa and others became leading advocates for preservation of the barrios at the time.

Community opponents formed coalitions with the residents of Lomas de Poleo in Ciudad Juárez who were also under siege by the Mexican profiteers. Protests were organized at both the Mexican and U.S. Consulate offices. Educational forums were held to inform the public about the damage caused to communities by the regional revitalization effort.

Paso del Sur was able to count on the support of Father Rafael García and Sacred Heart Parish, one of El Paso's most historic and beloved institutions and a trusted and long-standing mainstay of the three barrios. A historical mural was painted on church property by artists Francisco Delgado, Mauricio Olague and about fifty Bowie

High School students. The mural depicted revered barrio leaders contributing to community pride and solidarity.

Protests at city hall ensued regarding eminent domain resulting in council action to postpone its use. Downtown retail store owners, under the banner Land Grab Opponents, also organized and filed conflict of interest complaints against Councilman Beto O'Rourke, the son-in-law of Bill Sanders, founder of PDNG. The charges were later dismissed when he agreed to recuse himself on certain votes.[12]

Although the secret workings of the PDNG were reported on sporadically and superficially by local media, only *Newspaper Tree*, a local online news magazine, described the membership and their activities. It wasn't until May 2007 that *The Texas Observer* published an in-depth cover story (including potential conflicts of interest) titled "Eminent Disaster: A Cabal of Politicians and Profiteers Target an El Paso Barrio."

As a result of both the strong resistance of the community and the effects of the recession of the late 2000s, the plans to demolish Segundo Barrio were apparently abandoned. However, Duranguito, the smallest of the barrios, continued to be threatened as its location was viewed by PDNG as a prime site for a coveted downtown sports arena. Paso del Sur continued its vigilance.

Meanwhile, individual members and associates of PDNG were preparing to profit from revitalization by acquiring properties in Duranguito and downtown and by forming new business entities. For example, from 2005 to 2013, Paul Foster registered more than a dozen limited liability corporations, including Franklin Management JFC LLC, through which he partnered with C. F. "Paco" Jordan of Jordan Construction (in 2013).[13] JORDAN FOSTER signs at private and public construction sites in the city have become ubiquitous.[14] Significantly, Foster has become the largest landowner of downtown El Paso properties.

Other PDNG members bought properties in Duranguito knowing they would profit nicely when the city was ready to buy out the neighborhood.[15] These properties and several others were purchased by the city in 2017 in amounts double or triple their appraised values.[16] Thanks to open records requests, the contracts and outrageous amounts paid on these transactions were publicly disclosed.

Let the Taxpayers Pay for It

It is not known if public funding of the coveted sports arena was envisioned from the outset or if, during the process, PDNG realized how easy it was to take control of city government and get taxpayers to pay for it. After all, it is not uncommon for a monied group of private citizens who yearn for a sports arena in their city to pool their resources and build it themselves. Apparently, little thought was given to this possibility. Instead they convinced Mayor John Cook and the so-called progressive city representatives to not only support a downtown baseball park but to add an arena to the proposed Quality of Life Bond package of 2012. Manipulation of the ordinance language would go a long way to mislead the voters into approving a multi-project Quality of Life Bond package.[17]

Manipulation of the Ballot Language Pays Off

In 2012, the city was confronted with a challenge: how to convince voters to approve public bonds incurring millions of dollars in debt for a sports arena that many argued was not wanted or needed. Again Joyce Wilson took charge and, with the help of Leonard "Tripper" Goodman, arranged to hire a sports arena consultant, Rick Horrow, who had figured out the formula to convince voters into approving these kinds of measures.[18] Basically, the formula consisted of avoiding the use of certain words that taxpayers were averse to, like "sports arena." Also, Horrow recommended that several projects be "bundled together," i.e., the attractive with the undesirable, so that voters could not pick and choose. Finally, Horrow urged that the city promote the bond as an improvement of the "quality of life" of El Paso's residents, emphasizing families and children.[19]

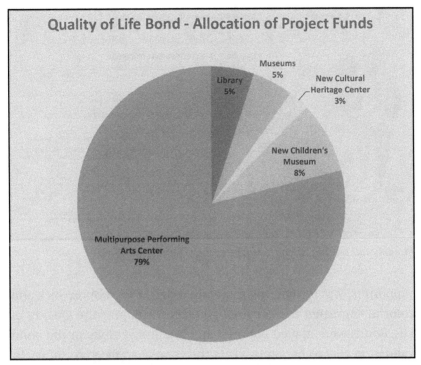

Quality of Life Bond - Allocation of Project Funds

Museums 5%

Library 5%

New Cultural Heritage Center 3%

New Children's Museum 8%

Multipurpose Performing Arts Center 79%

Source: City of El Paso

Perhaps one of the last official acts of the PDNG was the release of a press statement on September 13, 2012, announcing its support for the three propositions in the November bond election. After disbanding, the PDNG's leadership re-emerged as the Borderplex Alliance, also comprised exclusively of the super wealthy.[20] The Alliance presently drives the city's economic development efforts.

On September 29, 2012, the city council approved the bond ordinance and ballot language for the November 6, 2012 election. It contained three propositions: improvements to neighborhood parks and libraries; creation of three signature projects, a multipurpose cultural and performing arts center, a children's museum and a Hispanic Cultural Center; and funding for the baseball park with Hotel Tax revenues (HOT).

The El Paso Tomorrow PAC, headed by Mr. Goodman and other

Promotional brochures sent to voters. El Paso Tommorow PAC.

supporters, was formed to promote passage of the bonds. Slick and colorful campaign mailers urging voters to support the Quality of Life Bonds were mailed out and later became exhibits in the bond validation trial to help prove that the voters had received sufficient information about the projects.[22] These promotional materials also failed to make mention that the city was seeking approval for a sports arena! The bond election had a very low voter turnout but the bond was approved by a large margin (71 percent).[23] The city commenced implementing projects in Proposition 1 and 3. However, the city council took no action to implement the "multipurpose performing arts center" (AKA sports arena) and the cultural center for four years.

City Council Takes Aim at Duranguito

Between 2012 and 2016, the city contracted various consultants, architects and designers purportedly to recommend the best site for the downtown arena. Numerous media reports discussed the potential location of the arena; however, no official city council vote had been taken to decide the issue. On October 17, 2016, the city council finally selected the site deemed most suitable, which, not surprisingly, was the same site initially marked by SWMW on the 2006 "not-for-distribution map."[24] That site was Duranguito, El Paso's first platted neighborhood.

The decision had come down with no prior notice to the residents of Duranguito and with complete disregard not only for the opinions of historians but also neighborhood groups, civic associations, and other interested parties that had expressed support for preserving the historic neighborhood at numerous forums, including at city council meetings, where the opposition outnumbered support by ten to one.[25]

Needless to say, barrio supporters and preservationists reacted with anger and dismay and vowed to fight the city's plans to eradicate the historic residential area. Countless requests from Paso del Sur and from preservationists, including Dr. Max Grossman, an art history professor at UTEP, were made to city council to reconsider the location. Supporters of the barrio decided to engage in positive community action. Duranguito became the site of many neighborhood events, including musical performances, Bach in the Barrio, cultural festivals, Día de los Muertos, religious processions, and *posadas*—all supported by artists, musicians, Sacred Heart Catholic Church and other community organizations. Paso del Sur launched a citizen's petition drive which garnered more than six thousand signatures to designate Duranguito as a historic district. Later, another petition drive was conducted to request a re-vote of the bond election; this petition also garnered thousands of signatures. These citizen initiatives, however, were unsuccessful in forcing the city to reconsider or to put the matter before the voters.

At the end of December 2016, Mayor Oscar Leeser and several city representatives attempted to take action to change the arena site; however, they ran into potential violations of the Open Meetings Act. County officials called for investigations by the Texas Rangers and two of the participants in the meeting, Dr. Max Grossman and Bernie Sargent, lost their positions on the county's historical commission. Ultimately, no charges were filed, and no change was made to the location. Duranguito remained as the targeted site.[26]

The Fight is Taken to the Courts

The city, realizing the breadth and depth of the opposition, decided to act preemptively by filing an Expedited Declaratory Judgment action under Government Code: Chapter 1205, known as a bond validation lawsuit. The lawsuit was filed in Travis County rather than El Paso County. Numerous barrio and preservation advocates were interested in joining the litigation as respondents but could not do so due to prohibitive litigation costs. Two of the strongest advocates for preservation of the barrio filed as respondents, Dr. Max Grossman, who had the financial backing of a noted Texas preservationist,[27] Dr. Yolanda Leyva, who filed *pro se*, and several Duranguito residents, including Antonia "Toñita" Flores Morales, the lone resident tenant who refused the city's relocation money, as well as Candelaria García, Emily Sáenz Gardea, and Olga López, were represented by a legal team headed by local attorney Verónica Carbajal of Texas Rio Grande Legal Aid. Leonard Goodman, III, a strong proponent of revitalization and head of the Tomorrow PAC, entered the case as intervenor in support of the city.

A two-day bench trial was held in Austin on July 17 and 18, 2017. It was live-streamed by KVIA-TV. The citizen respondents contended the city always intended to build a sports arena but decided to request authorization for a "multipurpose performing arts facility" because the voters would not approve a sports arena. Just prior to the trial the city had issued an RFQ (request for qualifications) in which the facility was described as a basketball stadium. The most relevant and basic contention of the city at trial was that, referring to the language in the bond ballot, "multipurpose performing arts and entertainment," as a matter of law, includes sports and sporting events.[28] Respondent Grossman contended the bond proceeds could not be used to build a basketball arena because a basketball arena is not a performing arts facility authorized by the ordinance. Similarly, the Morales respondents contended that the text of the

City commits to restoring the Abraham Chavez Theatre.

bond ordinance limited expenditures to "library, museum, cultural and performing arts facilities," none of which include a facility that is designed or equipped to host sporting events.[29]

The Morales respondents also contended the cultural center was a mandatory project and should receive priority over the multipurpose performing arts facility. Under the bond language, the city was required to construct a new cultural center but it could either renovate the existing Abraham Chavez Theater or construct a new facility.

The trial court decided in favor of respondents on the multipurpose performing arts facility by issuing a decision forbidding the city to use bond proceeds to build a sports arena. Later the final judgment also restricted the city's use of non-bond funding to modify, complete or enhance the facility. The city and Morales respondents appealed

Tense moments during confrontation with EPPD.

the trial court's judgment to the Third Court of Appeals in Travis County. The Appeals Court reversed the trial court's judgment, ruling that the language of the bond allowed the city broad discretion to construct a sports arena.[30] The respondents then filed Petitions for Review to the Texas Supreme Court. No ruling has been made as of this writing (November 5, 2019).

Also pending in the courts is an action filed by Dr. Max Grossman on July 31, 2017, under the Texas Antiquities Act.[31] Grossman sought injunctive relief against the city to prevent the demolition of properties within Duranguito until the city complied with applicable notice to the Texas Historical Commission (THC).[32] The city argued that the requirements were inapplicable because the properties were private as the transactions to purchase the properties had not yet been finalized. Hundreds of protesters came out to the neighborhood when they heard bulldozers were setting up to raze the buildings. El Paso Police Officers were deployed and tension filled the air. Just in time, the Court of Appeals issued an emergency order requiring the city to cease and desist from demolishing the buildings.

Presence of bulldozers provokes Duranguito supporters. Photo by David Romo.

Bulldozers' Strike Inspire Advocacy of the Rebirth of the Neighborhood

Overnight all seemed well, however on September 12, 2017, at dawn, without notice or warning to anyone, bulldozers again rolled into Duranguito and punched gaping holes in five of the most important buildings. The city denied responsibility because the bulldozers were hired by the property owners. The residents, Paso del Sur, the litigants, and supporters were outraged. Supporters gathered in protest for the rest of the day and many days and weeks thereafter. Grossman's attorneys filed a second emergency injunction, this time requiring the city to cancel all demolition permits previously granted to property owners.

Paso del Sur members renewed their vow to support residents of Duranguito Toñita Morales and Romelia Mendoza, who had remained stalwart in their resolve to save their neighborhood. Upset and shaken by the sight of bulldozers and the unsightly damage caused to buildings, the Duranguito supporters promised to remain vigilant twenty-four hours a day to prevent any further damage to the buildings. And so a *plantón* or protest site, was set up on the sidewalk in front of the damaged buildings for an entire year, and activists and the few remaining residents stood watch 24/7.[33] Except for two arrests and a few citations, the numerous protests and other events were peaceful, drawing media attention and greater support for the movement to save Duranguito.

Barrio advocates, including historians and architects led by Dr. David Romo, had been working to develop an alternative plan to the city's plans for demolition and the construction of an arena. On December 15, 2018, J. P. Bryan, the preservationist from Houston and Max Grossman's supporter in the litigation, hosted a public forum on historic preservation, with state and national experts among the presenters. Dr. Romo spoke on the need to bring about the rebirth of Duranguito, visually depicting a beautifully preserved and restored neighborhood and highlighting all of its historic attributes.[34] Whether this visionary image or a sports arena will stand on this location in the future is still a question to be determined either by the courts or by political process.

In October 2018 while the cases were pending, a historian from Las Cruces, New Mexico, published a book, *A Good War and a Bad Peace*, in which he documented the presence of an Apache peace camp

"Old Town Duranguito." Paso del Sur Rebirth of Duranguito Project.

Flor de Luna building reimagined. Paso del Sur Rebirth of Duranguito Project.

in the area that is now Duranguito. This discovery compelled Max Grossman to file an injunction against demolition to insure Apache remains would be discovered, protected and preserved. The injunction was denied then appealed, thus remaining in effect as of this writing.

Conclusion

It should not have been a surprise that a downtown revitalization plan devised by wealthy private parties to raze entire blocks eradicating El Segundo and Duranguito would be met with anger and resistance. One might ask at this point, what went wrong? To be sure, PDNG members strongly believed they had come up with a masterful plan to transform the entire downtown from an old, worn out commercial zone that included blighted neighborhoods, to a vibrant, modern, upscale entertainment district where the well-heeled could come to spend their disposable income. Investing through publicly funded Quality of Life Bonds was an efficient and painless way to do it. Why would this plan be so controversial?

To begin with, the problem was that PDNG was comprised of

elites who were out of touch with the mainstream community of El Paso. They were able to convince many other well-to-do, prominent people, including impressionable civic leaders, that this was a grand project. Second, city government was weak; the mayor and council members had no plans of their own to spur economic development. They were courted, befriended and supported by the influentials and ultimately began representing them rather than their constituencies. Apparently, they were so convinced of the end that it justified the means. Third, the so-called partnership of movers and shakers and city council representatives misunderstood and underestimated barrio residents and community activists, not to mention the historic preservation community and supporters.

When a private group is perceived to wield more power than the elected representatives in a government that is supposed to be democratic, there is bound to be distrust and opposition. Accountability and transparency cannot be enforced and voters feel disenfranchised and rendered powerless. Decisions made in this manner cause divisions that will not easily mend, and the outcomes will be criticized and denounced well into the future. El Pasoans would be better served if elected representatives sought to understand the wants and needs of their true constituents and actually listened and considered citizen input and, in the process, provided true, accurate, and complete information regarding city plans and projects. Citizens, on the other hand, must become better informed about city government, knowing who is working behind the scenes, and who stands to benefit from certain decisions. Citizens must be engaged by joining civic organizations, attending city meetings and events and, of course, they must become conscientious voters.

II. The Baseball Park Boondoggle

OSCAR J. MARTÍNEZ[1]

In June, 2012, the El Paso City Council approved the building of a tax-supported baseball park to serve as the playing field for a Triple-A team which was about to be purchased by the MountainStar Sports Group (MSSG), a company founded in 2010 by Paul Foster, his wife Alejandra de la Vega Foster, and Woody Hunt. That decision created a furor. Critics objected to the pressure applied to the council by the MSSG owners to support their project, and even more to the council's exclusion of the public in the decision-making process. Opponents further balked at the $50 million price tag and the site chosen to build the stadium—where the El Paso City Hall and the Insights Science Museum stood. These buildings would need to be demolished to make room for the ballpark. Despite the protests, the MSSG owners got their project and the taxpayers got saddled with the bills. This essay narrates the story of one of the most contentious ventures undertaken by the city in collaboration with wealthy businesspeople.

Background

As pointed out in Carmen E. Rodríguez's piece on Duranguito (see Section I), in the early 2000s, entrepreneurs and developers William Sanders, Paul Foster, and Woody Hunt organized the Paso

Southwest University Park. Photo by author.

del Norte Group (PDNG), an exclusive consortium largely composed of influential El Pasoans and a select group of businesspeople from Ciudad Juárez, Mexico. The main intent of the PDNG was to revitalize downtown El Paso and other nearby locales. In 2006 the city council approved a PDNG plan that called for the building of a sports arena as part of an entertainment, arts, and shopping district in the greater El Paso downtown area. The idea of building an arena in downtown had been around at least since 1999, with boosters arguing that such a structure would be a catalyst for economic development. In 2000, then Mayor Carlos Ramírez had considered adding a $144 million arena to that year's Quality of Life Bond election but decided against it out of concern that it would generate so much opposition that other proposed bond items would be endangered.[2]

Rodríguez (see Section I) details how the 2006 PDNG/city council plan generated controversy because it left open the possibility that the city might use eminent domain to acquire buildings in the downtown area and also in the Mexican American neighborhoods known as Segundo Barrio and Duranguito (or the Union Plaza District) for the purpose of redevelopment. During 2006 and 2007, concerned citizens, including owners of downtown properties, spoke against the plan and sought legal recourse to fight the city's urban renewal scheme. Mexican Americans and others concerned with the possible disintegration of Segundo Barrio, including Chicano/a leaders, historical preservationists, and small business owners, held demonstrations and organized marches in which hundreds of people participated. They mostly objected to the proposal to demolish historic sites and apartment complexes. The idea of displacing poor Mexican Americans from their neighborhoods to make room for structures favored by profit-seeking businesspeople was especially galling to barrio activists.

As opposition mounted, the PDNG/city council's proposal of using eminent domain to acquire private properties faded into the background. But proponents persisted in attempting to transform the downtown area into a lively, chic district that young professionals (the "creative class") would frequent and eventually inhabit. As part of that vision, Foster, Hunt, and De la Vega, the MSSG owners, made known their desire to bring a Triple-A baseball team to El Paso. Thus, they promoted the notion that the city needed a brand-new stadium to spark economic development, elevate the town's profile, and improve the local "quality of life."

Was there really a need for a new baseball stadium? El Paso already had a perfectly suitable facility, Cohen Stadium, that could be renovated and used by a new team. Despite that, the MSSG and its supporters on the city council found the Cohen option unsatisfactory because that stadium was twenty-two years old—and it was located twelve miles from downtown. The MSSG owners insisted that the league required that the stadium be located downtown and the city council accepted that.

In the public mind, the idea of building a baseball stadium in the downtown area would bring to fruition the old infatuation for an "arena." But that turned out not to be the case. Downtown revitalizers would not be satisfied with just the baseball stadium; they would keep pressing hard for an additional sports venue, which they would continue to refer to informally as the "arena."

The Controversial Decision to Build the Baseball Stadium

To understand why the city approved the baseball stadium, it is important to keep in mind that for years elites had pushed the idea that the downtown area needed a sports venue. For example, the 2012 city report "Plan El Paso" reflected that obsession. The report recommended that one of the new downtown projects should be an "arena which would become a regional entertainment destination...envisioned to attract national and international events...." "The arena itself," continued "Plan El Paso," "would be flexible, containing 15,000–18,000 seats to accommodate local and regional sports teams, and offer conversion for large-scale cultural events and convention/exhibition uses." The plan identified three possible spots in the downtown area for the location of the new arena, including the space occupied by city hall and the Insights Science Museum.[3]

In 2012, while the idea of building a baseball stadium was being floated in the community, the city discussed a Quality of Life Bond ballot to present to the voters in the November 6, 2012, election. One of the propositions on the ballot would call for using hotel tax revenues to fund the baseball stadium. Another proposition sought voter support for the building of a "multi-purpose performing arts and entertainment" facility, deliberately avoiding the use of the words "arena" and "sports" to lessen voter objections. The scheme worked and the bond passed. Jubilant arena boosters claimed that the voters had indeed supported the arena, denying any intent to cause confusion with misleading vague ballot language. But any informed person easily understood the deception to which the voters had been subjected. (See Section I).

Another example of manipulation occurred during the promotional phase of the ballot initiative. The foremost concern among ballot promoters was to get voter approval for funding the baseball stadium and, at the same time, get consent for the "multi-purpose performing arts and entertainment" facility (the arena). At one point the city solicited input from citizens regarding their wants and desires to improve the local quality of life, including asking for online opinions and comments via note cards. The arena appeared on the list of options. Among the five thousand responses received, the preference for streetcars came in first, and the arena came in second. When the arena note cards were examined, however, it became obvious that 542 of them were not written by 542 different individuals, but rather by only one or two persons. An investigation by journalists into the scheme to turn in bogus cards revealed the involvement of individuals with connections to El Paso sports teams and the El Paso Tomorrow PAC, a PDNG offshoot organization that promoted the arena. The journalists also uncovered ties between a "card activist" and city bureaucrats. Whether knowledgeable or not about the ruse, city officials referenced those tainted cards to spread the message that the community strongly supported the building of a sports facility separate from the baseball stadium. The arena boosters said little about cheating or ballot stuffing.[4]

The confusion created by the disingenuous language in the bond ballot and the way it was promoted played to the advantage of the baseball park supporters. Foster and Hunt, who had been shopping for a Triple-A baseball team since 2010, suddenly announced that they were about to purchase the Tucson Padres. But, they asserted, the deal would not be consummated unless the city made a commitment to build a new, tax-supported baseball stadium for the team. The ball, so to speak, was thrust into the city council's court, and the representatives were told they had to act quickly because any delay would torpedo the accord.

A debate surfaced over whether the city council should rush to decide the stadium question. Within a matter of days, the true believers

Old city hall. Courtesy of the city of El Paso.

on the council indeed yielded to the investors' pressure and, on June 26, 2012, they voted six to two to build a $50-million stadium in the downtown area. The financing would come from hotel taxes, so it would be an easy sell to the voters because city residents would not have to pay for the stadium. Outsiders would be the ones paying the bills. Understandably, the hospitality community opposed the idea of saddling visitors with the high tax.

Even more controversial than the idea of building a baseball stadium for the convenience and benefit of the MSSG owners was the decision to sacrifice city hall and the Insights Science Museum, which catered to children, to make room for the facility. The council justified the destruction of the city hall building by saying that the building was not in a good location and needed repairs and upgrades, so it was best to level it. The children's science museum apparently was not doing well financially, and it occupied a much smaller building. Little thought was given to finding alternative sites for the stadium and to the prospect that, upon the destruction of city hall, city employees would necessarily be scattered in different buildings around the downtown area.

The Resistance

Those decisions shocked many El Pasoans. Mayor John Cook became the most vocal opponent to having the city assume the cost of building the new stadium. He threatened to veto the council vote, pointing out that decisions on quality-of-life issues should go to the voters, that it was not appropriate to channel hotel tax funds to the stadium, and that the planned demolition of city hall was a huge mistake. Cook stated that it would cost from $80 to $100 million to raze a perfectly good building (valued at $38 million) and then to have to purchase or lease and renovate older ones to house city offices. He rejected the claims by stadium advocates that the sports venue would become an economic catalyst and that it would eventually pay for itself; rather, Cook said, taxpayers would be the ones paying for the stadium and its maintenance for years to come.[5]

Lo and behold, two weeks after he threatened to veto the project, Cook did an about-face and expressed support for the stadium, explaining that he had acquired a better understanding of the funding mechanisms that the city council had put in place. He had assumed, he said, that the sale of tax bonds would be necessary to pay for the stadium if the voters rejected the proposal to raise the hotel tax. He learned, however, that approval of tax bonds for a stadium would need to come directly from the voters. Also, his veto could be overridden by six council votes, instead of seven, as he had thought. Many people believed that the real explanation for his flip flop was that he succumbed to the pressure applied by the backers of the stadium.[6]

Two former mayors, Larry Francis and Ray Salazar, and an ex-city planner, Nestor Valencia, condemned the stadium decision. On August 12, 2012, Francis published an editorial titled "City Hall Armageddon," in which he characterized the stadium as

> an absolutely disastrous idea that will lead to both a financial and a structural Armageddon to the detriment of our city for decades to come.... The economic and structural drain on city government and ultimately the taxpayers is horrendous. The list of problems with this

deal is massive and well-documented.... The investment percentages by the city versus the team owners are lopsided and unfair.... There is zero return or repayment by the team owners. Albuquerque gets about $700,000 rent per year [for its stadium] and a percentage of all concessions. We get $50,000 per year.... We are giving them [Foster, Hunt, and De la Vega] the stadium and parking garage for free. The most troubling aspects of this are the scattering of city government around town, the secrecy of the negotiations, the lack of disclosure to our citizens of the cost and impact, and an apparent deliberate attempt to conceal the whole process from our citizens. We can no longer trust city government.... As a former mayor, I would ask Paul Foster and Woody Hunt to step back and re-evaluate this entire deal. The burden on the city is much too one-sided.[7]

Former Mayor Ray Salazar followed up indignant comments he made against the stadium by filing a lawsuit to block the proposed tearing down of city hall. The lawsuit, which was unsuccessful, alleged that some city officials had misused public resources to carry out the stadium project.[8]

Former City Planner Nestor Valencia wrote in an editorial that, heretofore, the city had always let voters decide whether to endorse or disapprove of proposed expensive projects such as the ballpark:

This is clearly a quality of life project and as such should be placed before the voters of El Paso. Council failed in its responsibility to its constituency. This project needs voter consent. Another major flaw is the complete lack of adequate planning, lack of alternate stadium sites to be considered, demolition of city hall, and the lack of an adequate plan to relocate City Hall resulting in the scattering of city functions at random. It destroys the purpose of Cohen Stadium. This process makes no public administration or business sense. It also nullifies the purpose of General Obligation funding through voter referendums. **The citizens of El Paso are not interested in micro-managing the day-to-day operations of city affairs. They are concerned when a large sum of taxpayer dollars is on the table. Council's responsibility is to listen to the people and protect the interest of the public** [my emphasis].[9]

Demolition of city hall. Courtesy of the city of El Paso.

In addition to the stinging rebuke by past government officials, council members who voted for the stadium faced hundreds of enraged citizens at community meetings. In one gathering, when asked how audience members would have voted if given a chance, almost everyone indicated they would have voted against the stadium. One speaker expressed the frustration and anger felt by many that the council had failed to put the stadium issue before the voters; instead, it arrogantly made an expensive decision without public input.[10] Council members who voted for the stadium defended themselves by saying that the ballpark presented a unique opportunity to revitalize a "decaying" downtown area, and that the city hall building was not in good condition and needed to be replaced.[11]

Despite the public outcry, the council decision stuck. Thus, the baseball stadium became a done deal months before the "quality of life" November 6 bond election would take place. The scheme concocted by local power brokers in collaboration with city representatives worked. The voters indeed approved the bond ballot. But the devious interpretation of arena boosters that the city should now proceed to build another facility where sports activities could be held created a public uproar and led to one of the longest disputes in El

Paso's history. Citizens who were not only opposed to the notorious arena, but also to the razing of Duranguito, the Mexican American neighborhood where the city had chosen to build the facility, spoke out angrily at council meetings, held marches and demonstrations and, most importantly, challenged the city's plan in the courts, with lawsuits making their way to the Texas Supreme Court. As of the end of 2019, the arena project remained legally stalled. (See Section I).

Conclusion

The baseball park boondoggle in El Paso epitomizes the result of alliances that often form between wealthy businesspeople and city officials for the purpose of implementing projects that provide gains for some but are of limited value to taxpayers, who get stuck with the bills. In their excellent study of stadium building, Kevin J. Delany and Rick Eckstein conclude that, "the process of building private stadiums with public dollars...is more akin to plutocracy than democracy." They note that in Pittsburgh and Phoenix, where the locals did not want their taxes spent on sports facilities, "powerful stadium advocates...trampled on public sentiment and built stadiums anyway."[12] Much the same can be said for El Paso.

In El Paso, the MSSG, led by Paul Foster and Woody Hunt, persuaded the city council to build a facility to house the Triple-A team that MSSG had picked to bring to the city. That decision committed taxpayers to assume unwanted debt. In March 2019, the city's chief financial officer predicted that the debt would be paid off by 2021, but to many observers that seemed overly optimistic.[13]

As predicted by critics, the ballpark has been operating at a deficit, with money taken from the city's general fund to make up for shortfalls. Precious tax dollars have been diverted from badly needed social and educational programs to pay for a non-essential sports facility in one of the poorest cities in the country. According to UTEP professor Dr. Max Grossman, through 2018 the cost of the ballpark, associated expenditures, and subsidies had amounted to $156 million, more than triple the $50 million originally earmarked by the city for the project. "Mind you," adds Grossman, "the $156 million figure does not include legal and administrative costs, the added cost of operating five city hall facilities instead of one, the added parking costs for city employees, and several other factors. It also does not include the cost of diverting police officers and their squad cars to baseball games for hundreds of hours per year.[14]

Claims that the ballpark would spur economic development have not materialized. Economic development means generating industries that pay high wages and salaries, and the ballpark has produced none of that. Temporary construction employment and part-time vendor and usher jobs do not constitute economic development. In an article entitled "Welfare for Team Owners," a national magazine points out that many studies indicate that there is "no discernible positive relationship between sports facility construction and local economic development, income growth, or job creation."[15]

III. Political Contributions: The Best Candidates Money Can Buy?

KATHLEEN (KATHY) STAUDT [1]

El Paso's city elections have become extraordinarily expensive, probably beyond the reach of almost all El Pasoans as candidates unless they either generate contributions from wealthy patrons or mobilize a massive grassroots campaign. Who invests in successful candidates? Are El Pasoans governed under a "pay-to-play" system? To what extent do political investments from wealthy contractors, builders, and land moguls reap benefits, short-term and long-term, for their business interests? The answer to the last question cannot be answered in this brief article, but mostly Anglo/White[2] wealthy donors' access to power and visions for, let's say a remodeled downtown, a decision-maker hire in city hall, or a friendly climate for their interests are likely served in their political campaign donations.

Fortunately, we can easily access information about who donates to candidates running for office. Texas ethics laws require that candidates provide the names, employers of donors, and the amounts of cash or in-kind contributions donated to their campaigns on specific dates. These details are publicly posted on the city of El Paso's Municipal Clerk's website.[3] Neither El Paso nor Texas sets caps on campaign contributions to state and local candidates. As is clear from the evidence presented in this essay, big-money donations overwhelmingly come from wealthy Anglo El Pasoans in this largely Mexican American city. Most of the big donors probably vote Republican in El Paso, a place where 60 percent or more of voters support Democratic candidates—suggesting a disconnect between the governed and politicians who represent them.

The information in this essay tabulates different aspects of campaign donations for those who sit on the current city council in 2019. Voters should question whether these contributions lead primarily to outcomes that benefit large donor interests; as an old adage goes, "follow the money." Nonvoters allow those who do vote—a small percentage of the population—to elect candidates and thereby perpetuate the ease by which big money influences city government.

Governance in El Paso

The city charter, like a constitution for states or bylaws for nonprofit organizations, consists of rules about the basic structure of government. El Pasoans, living in eight geographic districts, elected our current mayor and council with the expectation that they represent the diversity of El Paso's population. Candidates are elected on a non-partisan basis (that is without political party identification) unlike in other levels of government: county, state, and beyond.

In 2004, considered late for large cities, El Paso finally adopted a City Manager System to govern. She managed the city with an assistant city manager. The current city manager has five members on his "Executive Team," three of them deputy city managers reporting to him in a growing bureaucracy. His salary was $315,000 in 2017.[4]

The mayor and city council representatives may serve a maximum of two four-year terms. For those who wish to run as an incumbent for a second and final term, an incentive exists to develop not only good responsiveness to their constituents but also relationships with multiple donors in order to generate contributions to finance their second campaign.

Over the last fifteen years, El Paso has experienced a tremendous rise in the cost of campaigns. These high costs make it difficult for

most people to consider a run for office. And some city council candidates refuse to attend forums and face the voters, based on advice from their paid political consultants, as long as they get large monetary donations for mailers and billboards.

Since 2003, the first year data was posted on the municipal website, the cost of campaigns has doubled to almost $400,000 for the current mayor alone.[5] Moreover, shifts have occurred in the names of big donors and the size of their contributions. For example, big donors once rarely invested sums of $2,500, but nowadays, multiple donations from multiple members of families run up to $10,000 and more. These sizeable amounts are legal, but some might question whether they are ethical.

Mayor Margo

The following list contains surnames of the top-twenty donors to Mayor Donald (Dee) Margo's 2017 campaign. Only four of the donors (in bold) have Spanish surnames in a city that is 83 percent Hispanic according to the latest census figures. Mayor Margo has a broad numerical base of almost five hundred donors for the total of $378,315 raised. A sum like this, we can assume, puts a run for mayor outside the realm of most middle-income and working-class people. NOTE that *multiple first names* are associated with these surname totals. The top-ten donors generated a quarter of the mayor's total sum, while the top-twenty donors amounted to over a third (36 percent) of the total.

Top-Twenty Donors to Mayor Margo's 2017 Campaign

1.	Foster, multiple first names	$23,500 (+$2,358 in kind)
2.	EP Trade School Inc., multiple first names (Kuykendall, Terrell)	$15,000
3.	Rogers, multiple first names	$11,500
4.	Wakefield	$10,000
5.	Randag	$10,000
6.	Chiu	$7,000
7.	Hunt, multiple first names	$6,000 (+$2,635 in kind)
8.	Cardwell, multiple first names	$6,000
9.	Margo III	$6,000
10.	Schwartz, multiple first names	$5,000
11.	**Paredes**	$5,000
12.	Tx Assoc Realtors PAC	$5,000
13.	Estes (ex-senator, Denton, TX)	$5,000
14.	Robison	$5,000
15.	Dudley	$5,000
16.	**Domínguez**	$4,854 (in-kind)
17.	**Fernández**, multiple first names	$4,900
18.	Interstate Commerce, Eisenberg & Furman	$4,752
19.	**Guerra**	$4,000
20.	Lowenfield	$4,000

(For the remaining donors, readers should consult the municipal clerk's website. One could categorize donors by other funding amounts, such as medium-sized contributions, $1,500–$3,900; smaller-sized, $500–$1,400; and smallest-sized, under $500.)

As we see, several donors contributed $10,000 or more, with the Foster surname at the helm. Paul Foster is a philanthropist-businessman in the business fields of contracting, building, and land development which benefit from public investments. He is also well known for his vision of downtown and his contribution for the Texas Tech Paul Foster Medical School.

Remember, eight representatives serve on El Paso's City Council, for which five votes constitute a majority to pass ordinances, resolutions, and evaluations of major personnel. The mayor only votes in a four-to-four tie and can veto legislation.[6] However, the mayor exerts power in various other ways, including as presiding officer at official meetings, as a representative of El Paso in intergovernmental meetings, as spokesman before the media, and in his use of the "bully pulpit." The last power has become somewhat controversial with the 2019 city Code of Conduct for elected officials, board members, and volunteers that forbids elected officials to speak "off the record" to the media. Some have called this a "gag rule" that inhibits constitutionally-protected free speech.

City Council Representatives: Varying Dependence on Big Donors

Big donors do not only invest campaign donations in their own district, or the districts of their businesses, but often donate in several other districts. Why? Each council representative casts a vote, so it is important to amass a majority of five or more votes for matters in which people have an interest. And incumbents who wish to run for a second term know that donors monitor the decision-making processes for issues of interest to them.

The following list shows the percentage of total donations to city council representatives coming from donors of $1,000 or more in the order of their dependency on big donors. We can assume that those representatives with low dependency on big donors are more likely to run grassroots campaigns with an emphasis on door-to-door, face-to-face campaigning, including presence at forums and debates. To the right is a map of district boundaries from the city website, with the diagonal lines referring to military installations.

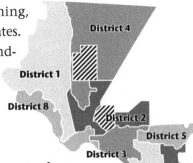

Donations to City Council Representatives: High-to-low dependency on big donors of $1,000+

District 5: 73 percent (Ordaz, total raised $50,650)
District 8: 64 percent (Lizárraga, total raised $133,757)
District 5: 59 percent (Salcido, total raised $46,672)
District 1: 55 percent (Svarzbein, total raised $127,265)
District 4: 48 percent (Morgan, total raised $24,955)
District 7: 43 percent (Rivera, total raised $21,059)
District 3: 39 percent (Hernández, $45,924)
District 2: 33 percent (Annello, total raised $12,861)

As shown from the list, big donors range from funding a high of 73 percent of total campaign finance (almost three-fourths) to a low of 33 percent (a third) of total campaign finance. Total campaign amounts also vary from over $12,000 to over $100,000. Several big donors contributed multiple times to single and multiple representatives who won office. The incumbent mayor Margo also donated to several city council representatives.

For council representatives' campaigns, the Hunt surname (with multiple first-name members) is at the helm totaling $22,500, in contrast to Foster as the biggest donor surname for mayor, with the Foster surname contributions to representatives totalling $12,500. Hunt Companies, on its website, says that it has "built more military homes on more military installations than any other developer,"[7] so the political climate for land, construction, and building is of business interest. The Hunt Family Foundation is also a major philanthropic donor in El Paso.[8] It should be noted that the El Paso Police Officers Association is in the big-donor category of multiple donations of $2,500 or more to multiple candidates; also active are the El Paso Fire Fighters and the El Paso Sheriff Deputies.

El Paso's council representatives are a diverse, gender-balanced group, but the campaign finance numbers raise questions about how much some may be beholden to big donors, especially when we look at other case study sections in this book.

Conclusions and Recommendations

Representative city government relies on victorious candidates who appeal to a broad cross-section of constituents and their interests. From the evidence presented in this section, one could infer that some representatives are beholden to the long-term business interests of big donors, particularly if and when they seek to run for re-election and generate similar amounts of support from the same donors. And given donors' multiple donations to multiple candidates, it is not surprising when council votes in near-consensus about important issues, such as big-money issues to develop parts of the city and/or to grant tax abatements and other incentives to builders and investors (see Section IV).

El Paso could place a cap on the size of campaign donations. An ordinance placing a cap of perhaps $400 per person would be ideal, but if politics is the "art of the possible," perhaps such an ordinance is unlikely to pass at this time. The city of Austin developed such a cap, adopted five years ago, which increases slightly from election to election. A $2,700 individual contribution to congressional campaigns existed in the 2016 election.[9]

Considering political arts of the possible, other approaches may be in order. One approach would be to make campaign finance an important ethical issue in the next election, with questions and concerns raised about big donors. Another would be to ask candidates at various public forums to PLEDGE that they will only accept donations under a particular amount, such as $400. Candidates DO need money to run campaigns, so voters should consider making small campaign donations to those they support (even a key presidential candidate in 2018 generated contributions from many people that averaged under $20!). For greater impact on local elections, community-based political action committees (PACS) could be formed to counter large individual donations. Candidates must also abide by conflict-of-interest rules and recuse themselves from decision-making when they might benefit from a council vote. It appears unseemly for the mayor to be a big donor for city council candidates.

Finally, a long-term strategy might involve restoring partisanship to city elections. As far back as a century ago in the U.S., local city elections, once partisan, underwent reforms to become more professional —deemed nonpartisan—than party elections. Nevertheless, political parties are mediating institutions that provide ways for voters to assess candidates' broad ideological and public policy issues as to whether their interests are served or not. As other sections of this book suggest, the connections between money, issues, and benefits appear to be oriented toward providing advantages to particular groups, many of them big donors and their business interests. Non-partisan elections may offer a deceptive front for elite-dominated elections.

Voter turnout is extraordinarily low in El Paso compared to other cities on both the U.S. and Mexico sides of the border—lower than any city or *municipio* in the fourteen cities and towns along the U.S.-Mexico border.[10] And El Paso is located in a state ranked near the bottom (#47!) among U.S. states in voter turnout.[11] Additionally, various efforts have been made to suppress voter turnout in Texas both historically and in contemporary times.

Voters should take seriously their responsibility to cast ballots for candidates who represent their interests as well as the public interest. When El Paso voters share enthusiasm and knowledge about an issue or a candidate, such as they did for the Lost Dog Trail 2019 issue, with its 89 percent support from voters (see Section VII), or the 2018 U.S. Senate Campaign in Texas, they can win.

Now that local elections occur alongside other elections in November, voters face less fragmentation and have a greater ability to vote for candidates who will work for their interests, open their doors to access, and provide constituency services, voice, and access in between elections. Rather than elect the best candidates money can buy, let us select them based on the extent to which they serve districts and the broader public interest.

IV. El Paso's Public Debt Obligations v. "Quality of Life"

ROSEMARY NEILL
& KATHLEEN (KATHY) STAUDT[1]

In a well-managed government in a market economy, we would expect "private risk for public gain," rather than "public risk [like bond debts] for private gain." El Paso city government has opted for the latter, thereby saddling unhealthy debt obligations on its taxpayers.

In 2012, El Paso voters supported the vaguely worded Proposition 2, one of three propositions in the Quality of Life Bond that would create more parks and entertainment, an improved zoo and library, and a Mexican American Cultural Center among other items. In the bond election, the issue framing was misleading. The city's post-election decision to locate an arena in Duranguito without assessing the destructive impact on that neighborhood is a prime example (see Section I).

Voters may not have realized that bonds are long-term loans—debts which taxpayers repay with interest. Whether people voted or not, they were, are, and will be, obligated to repay the loans. Part of the city's claim and rationale for laying out bond propositions involved both so-called quality-of-life improvements for residents and perhaps the attraction of more people to settle in El Paso. Attracting more residents is important because unlike other municipalities, El Paso's assessed value of taxable property relies heavily on resi-

dential property. Of the total actual 2018 value of over $38 billion, 64 percent of assessed taxable value came from residential property, 29 percent from commercial property and 7 percent from industrial property, according to the El Paso Central Appraisal District.

This means that residents carry a disproportionate property tax burden and feel the sting of high property taxes, especially for the costliest line item on their property tax bill: school districts. But the second costliest item is the city. The city has long hoped and expected that an increase in downtown property tax values would shift some of the tax burden away from residents. On a sporadic basis, the city has also worked to expand housing development through smart growth inside the city rather than adding to the infrastructure-intensive sprawl of the county (see Section VII). Little did people realize that:

- the city council would provide generous tax incentives to relieve new businesses from paying their share of the tax burden for five to ten years in order to entice them to settle in El Paso and create jobs, even with such minimal salaries as $11/hour for the vast majority of employees.[2]

- the city would subsidize for-profit businesses by offering public bond money in formal and informal partnerships, such as the ballpark (see Section II), with risky ventures that might never pay off without more public subsidies.

Debt Trends: El Paso v. Other Texas Cities

The Texas State Comptroller's office provides an excellent resource for city residents to assess whether their local government is well managed or perhaps headed toward a financial crisis. The website considers factors such as median income, current debt obligations, population growth (presumably producing an expanded property tax base), and per capita (per person) rates to show debt trends and to compare debt outstanding with other cities of a similar size.

El Paso's tax-supported debt as of August 31, 2017, was over a billion dollars (that is a b for billion, not an m for million!), or more precisely, $1,254.2 million with a per capita tax-supported debt of $1,835 based on its (slow-growing) population of 683,577. The per capita debt obligations of Austin, Fort Worth, and Arlington were all less than El Paso as shown in Table 1 (on following page).

From 2008 to 2017, El Paso's debt trend increased by 54 percent, while its population during that same period grew by only 9 percent. Only in two cities (Lubbock and Garland, both less than 250,000 in population) are per capita tax-supported debts higher. (Note that the site contains a disclaimer that the data—from the Texas Bond Review Board and the U.S. Census—have not been independently verified.)

The comptroller's information focused on tax-supported debt information. When one accounts for revenue bonds, loans, capital lease obligations, Chapter 380 Agreements and other forms of debt, the city's debt as of August 31, 2018, is more than $2.225 billion![3]

Other big cities in Texas, besides being home to large corporations

Table I. How El Paso Compares
Tax-supported Debt Outstanding for Cities of Similar Size, as of August 31, 2017

City Name	Tax-supported Debt Outstanding	Tax-supported Debt Outstanding Per Capita	Population
Austin	$1,465,564,994	$1,542	950,715
Fort Worth	$725,685,000	$830	874,168
El Paso	$1,254,200,000	$1,835	683,577
Arlington	$382,735,000	$966	396,394
Corpus Christi	$474,810,000	$1,458	325,605
Plano	$357,330,000	$1,249	286,143
Laredo	$300,340,000	$1,152	260,654
Lubbock	$1,047,295,000	$4,125	253,888
Irving	$440,055,000	$1,831	240,373
Garland	$463,205,000	$1,946	238,002

SOURCE: https://comptroller.texas.gov/transparency/local/debt/city.php?city
name=El+Paso&citysubmit=GO

and far higher median incomes, attract more people and grow their populations. In a growing population, people are likely to purchase more homes, thus expanding the property tax base, and to purchase more taxable goods (generating revenue from sales tax). According to the Texas Comptroller's site, the city property tax rate in 2017 was $0.803433. The proposed rate in 2018 went up to $0.847470 (between 84–85 cents per $100 property value). Then, in 2019, 59 percent of voters supported another bond of over $413 million.

Besides paying heavy school and city taxes, El Pasoans also receive property tax bills from the County of El Paso, the University Medical Center, and the El Paso Community College. El Paso's growth is slow to stagnating. One might ask: Why?

Residents Leave for Better Wages Elsewhere

Apart from its burdensome property tax rates, El Paso continues to experience a "brain drain." University graduates with degrees in STEM fields (science, technology, engineering, and math) leave for cities with better salaries especially in the private sector. El Paso has no major industries to absorb graduates, especially in the STEM fields. Perhaps the business community has not done its fair share to recruit and retain graduates with competitive salaries.

A shift may be occurring among El Paso's officials and business leaders. The state agency, Workforce Solutions Borderplex, the business group for education known as the Council on Economic Expansion and Educational Development (CREEED), and the El Paso Collaborative for Academic Excellence have put into place efforts to target upper salary quartile job creation. Begun in 2019, this precedent-setting collaboration is promising. However, the starting salaries for the upper quartile begin at just over $12 per hour, hardly comparable with the $15 legal minimum wage in place in various U.S. cities and states.[4] One might wonder why the upper-quartile salary is not higher.

A Race to the Bottom on "Quality of Life"?

City officials have begun to worry about their flawed strategy. In preparing the city's 2020 budget, the chief financial officer proposed closures for libraries, recreation centers and pools.[5] Simultaneously, and, ironically, given the water problems in the desert region, the city proclaims new quality-of-life water playgrounds. (See the picture in this link.[6]) Which will it be? Closing existing pools or opening new ones? Why is the city building new facilities if it cannot maintain existing facilities, and how does that dysfunction affect our quality of life?

The city is expecting its departments to retrench while it is adding additional debt. In the data from the city's Comprehensive Annual

Financial Report, the city's debt service in 2009 was $31,052,868 in principal and $34,187,775 in interest for a total of $65,240,643. By comparison, the combined Library ($8,446,529) and Parks Department ($18,751,833) expenditures for that year were $27,187,362. By 2018 our debt service expenditure was $57,199,348 for principal and $58,896,511 for interest for a total of $116,095,859. The net increase from 2009 to 2018 was $50 million.

The city is currently under a hiring freeze while it contemplates how it will manage its finances moving forward. As more debt is added, more must be set aside for debt service. As the cost of debt service rises, the amount available for routine budgetary needs falls. Recently passed state legislation that caps local government budget growth to 3.5 percent without voter approval will only add to the city's budgetary constraints.

Budgets: Who Rules Over Them?

We know that budget issues are tough. Information is diffused, difficult to interpret and reported in different fiscal periods. People's eyes glaze over at the thought of unpacking documents, revenue, expenditures, and debt service. To maintain transparent governance under these circumstances is an acute challenge. With the promise of adding jobs, well-connected business developers also use tools at the state level to establish, for example, special districts such as the recently proposed and passed "Municipal Management District No. 1, providing authority to issue bonds and to impose assessments, fees, or taxes." While jobs may be created, the long-term debt burden would continue to prevail.

El Paso's budget book for Fiscal Year 2020 is 596 pages long, not likely to attract all the readers that it should. Even if they read it, what influence will El Pasoans have?[7] The city website asked us to "chime in" on its website for comments that disappeared thereafter (results will be reported to city council, the city website says).[8] We hope the mayor and city council read and understand the budget and its ominous implications for El Paso's present quality of life and future solvency.

Conclusions and Recommendations

El Pasoans' quality-of-life projects and the obligations they impose must be understood both in contemporary and future time periods. Debt obligations are crowding out funding for basic services. City representatives, managers, and bureaucrats owe it to us, the public, to maintain existing services.

Additionally, debt clouds the hopes and visions about the city's future. Why? Overwhelming per person debt service may cast doubts on whether the city will remain solvent in the next decades, especially if the risky private-public partnerships do not produce gains for residents in terms of sustainable quality-of-life improvements. The downtown entertainment venues, from which private businesses are supposed to profit, have yet to provide a payoff to the city's revenue-generation efforts. Some of the venues may be priced outside the pocketbooks of mainstream El Pasoans who ultimately "vote with their feet" as young graduates have done: fleeing from heavy property tax burdens amid low wages and limited professional advancement opportunities.

The city needs to reconsider both taking on more debt and the provision of tax incentives and abatements that only perpetuate the extreme imbalance of residential property taxpayers' obligations compared to business and industry. The jobs created with tax incentives offer average wages lower than the minimum wage in many cities around the country. The city should set goals and timetables for lowering the residential property tax burden to 50 percent or less of the total property tax burden. The city and its voters should also put a moratorium on increasing debt obligations that pit current quality-of-life services against future ones. Voters need to force conversations on how we manage our debt load and the financial implications of further borrowing.

V. The Controversial Selection of Dr. Heather Wilson as UTEP President

OSCAR J. MARTÍNEZ[1]

In early March 2019, the University of Texas Board of Regents (hereafter Regents), named Dr. Heather Wilson, the then-Secretary of the U.S. Air Force and a former U.S. Congressperson (Republican), business consultant/lobbyist, and short-term president of a small technical university, as the next president of the University of Texas at El Paso (UTEP). The appointment provoked a furor among many El Pasoans due to Dr. Wilson's past controversial voting record, anti-LGBTQ policies, questionable consulting practices, no teaching background, and minimal experience in higher education administration.

On- and off-campus critics blamed powerful economic elites on the search committee for imposing an academically unqualified and controversial public figure on a large Hispanic-serving university whose student body is nearly 80 percent Mexican American, and, in addition, enrolls over one thousand students from Mexico. The population of El Paso, which is about 83 percent Mexican-origin people, closely parallels that of the university. These demographics were ignored in the selection of Dr. Wilson, giving rise to numerous questions, especially among Mexican Americans.

What major considerations drove Wilson's appointment? Obviously, this was a non-traditional decision. Was she picked because

Dr. Heather Wilson. Courtesy Luis Hernández.

of her potential usefulness to the business community in El Paso and elsewhere in Texas? Was she perceived as someone likely to put UTEP assets at the disposal of local leaders for the purpose of stimulating growth in the region? Was she chosen to further enhance the control of Republicans, who dominate politics in Texas, over higher education institutions in the state? Was the Regents' intent to select someone who could facilitate the spread of conservative ideological thinking among college students in El Paso?

Because answers to such questions have not been forthcoming from those who chose Dr. Wilson, some educated reasoning and informed speculation are in order regarding the role played by the most influential people who took part in the search process. Unfortunately for the public at large, the system of selecting university presidents in Texas has become much less democratic. Whereas in the past the Regents followed the standard open selection process

UTEP campus. Courtesy The Prospector.

used by universities across the country to appoint presidents, secretive and exclusive procedures now prevail. Wealth and politics more than ever play a decisive role in the determination of the types of candidates that are acceptable to those power brokers who currently select state university presidents.

The Regents Dismiss Requests from Mexican American Leaders

In the fall 2018, the Regents formed a Search Advisory Committee to make recommendations for a replacement for then-UTEP President Dr. Diana Natalicio, who had announced her retirement during the previous summer. People in the Mexican American community in El Paso immediately began thinking of the need to fill the vacancy with an educator who had the background and experience to function well in the unique bilingual, bicultural border environment of El Paso. They noted that UTEP had never been led by a person of Mexican/Hispanic heritage, someone who looked like most of the students, who spoke Spanish, and who shared their life experience.

Anticipating the impending formation of the search committee, in August 2018, twenty-eight Mexican American community leaders from a variety of professional backgrounds expressed their collective sentiments in a statement that addressed the kind of educator they felt UTEP required. Acting as the spokesman for the group, I sent the statement via an email to Dr. Steven Leslie, the Executive Vice Chancellor of the UT System and the person charged with organizing the committee and coordinating the search process. Dr. Leslie acknowledged receipt of the document and indicated he would share it with the Regents and the search committee.

In their statement, the twenty-eight Mexican Americans, most of them UTEP graduates, offered their help with the identification and evaluation of candidates, and requested that three at-large Mexican American community representatives be added to the search committee. The statement also specified basic qualifications, skills, and experience considered significant for the new UTEP president to have in order to successfully address the educational needs of a campus whose students were predominantly Mexican Americans. Below are key recommendations contained in the document; such suggestions coincided with thinking among UTEP faculty expressed to the committee as well.

- Academic administrative experience in a senior role such as university provost or vice president for academic affairs
- Commitment to the unique mission of a border-based university
- Experience and commitment to international education, global reach, study abroad, international student recruitment, and foreign language education
- Demonstrated commitment to diversity among faculty and administrators
- Experience in a Hispanic-serving institution
- Proficiency in Spanish strongly preferred
- Bicultural in U.S.-Mexico border community context

As it turned out, given the eventual selection of Dr. Wilson, an un-known number of members of the search committee—and ultimately the Regents—ignored the above criteria, even though the job an-nouncement in general did include similar desired qualifications. The Regents also disregarded the request that three Mexican Amer-ican at-large community delegates be added to the committee. The official "community" representatives appointed by the Regents to the committee turned out to be seven prominent business people, six from El Paso—Paul Foster (a Regent), Woody Hunt (a former Regent), Mayor Dee Margo, Renard Johnson, Sally Hurt-Deitch, and Edward Escudero, and one from Houston—Mike Loya, who had ties to El Paso. Others on the committee included Regents, presidents of other UT campuses, UTEP faculty and administrators, and a UTEP student and an alumnus. That lineup raised serious concerns that Foster, Hunt, and Margo, three wealthy and politically influential El Pasoans, would dominate proceedings and steer the selection of candidates their way.

Was Dr. Wilson's Appointment Politically Motivated?

In early March 2019, when Dr. Wilson was announced as the sole finalist for the UTEP presidency, suspicions surfaced immediately that Foster, Hunt, and Margo were Wilson's main promoters. All three are high-profile backers of the Republican Party in a state whose government has been dominated by Republicans for decades. Both Foster and Hunt have been big donors to the Republican Party and Republican candidates, and both had served on the Republican-laden Board of Regents, with Foster serving as past chairman and acting as vice-chairman at the time the UTEP decision was made. Again, using educated reasoning and informed speculation, it is not far-fetched to conclude that Foster, with backing from Hunt and Margo, played the pivotal role in persuading the Regents to first pick Dr. Wilson as the sole finalist and then unanimously confirm her as the new UTEP president.

Dr. Wilson's selection substantiated the misgivings about the search process initially communicated by the twenty-eight Mexican American leaders, as well as the suspicions conveyed by several community persons at UTEP on October 2, 2018, the day the search committee held its only public meeting. At that gathering, which was attended by campus and community people, the speakers made known their opposition to the overrepresentation of business interests on the committee, decried the exclusion of Mexican American at-large community representatives, protested the secretive manner in which the search would be conducted, and denounced the confining of the evaluation of candidates solely to the committee and the Regents. The community spokespersons further objected to the Regents' prerogative of either choosing a finalist from candidates submitted by the committee, or totally ignoring those recommendations and making their own selection. To many observers, the top-down, exclusionist, and secretive rules and procedures of the search process looked like a sham.

The stacking of the committee with powerful businesspersons and the expected receptiveness of the Board of Regents to a candidate with conservative credentials had its anticipated result—the appointment of Dr. Wilson, a right-wing politician/consultant/bureaucrat and latecomer to the world of higher education. Wilson had represented New Mexico in the U.S. Congress as a Republican (1998–2009), operated a consulting firm (2009–2013), had run unsuccessfully for the U.S. Senate (2011–2012), served as president of the South Dakota School of Mines and Technology (2013–2017), and (in 2017) secured an appointment in the Trump Administration as the U.S. Secretary of the Air Force, a position she held until May 31, 2019.

Reaction to Dr. Wilson's Appointment in the Community

Dr. Wilson's selection surprised—and shocked and angered—many El Pasoans, especially Mexican Americans who had expected that a

Latino or Latina educator would finally be named to the position. Why would the interests and desires of the majority population in El Paso, and on campus, be rejected so blatantly? How could the search committee and the Regents stray so far from the well-established practice of choosing university presidents from the ranks of career scholars/administrators who possessed ample experience in higher education? And how could they choose a political figure who had an ultra-conservative voting record and whose questionable consulting activities had for years been rebuked by ethical watchdog organizations? To the community, the Wilson choice added up to a political appointment of a nationally known Republican by well-placed local and Texas Republicans.

Critics, in particular members of the Community First Coalition, a confederation of twenty community organizations in El Paso, pointed out that Wilson's meager background in higher education did not prepare her to run a large, Mexican American-centered university like UTEP. Wilson speaks no Spanish and has paltry knowledge or acquaintance with borderlands Mexican heritage history and culture. After her stint in the U.S. Congress, she led a small, technical institution in South Dakota with 2,800 students, 86 percent of whom are of white European American descent. How could she leapfrog into a Carnegie-classified Research 1 institution of 25,000 students who are overwhelmingly of ethnic minority background? Further, Wilson has never served as a faculty member, a departmental chairperson, a dean, a vice president or provost. At universities, these experiences are essential for anyone who aspires for the highest-level decision-making position in which critical judgments are made about teaching, research, and tenure.

Equally as troubling, her votes in the U.S. Congress and her ratings from mainstream education, civil rights, and environmental groups reveal a protracted record of ultra-conservative interests and values that clash sharply with the progressive interests and values of most UTEP students and most El Pasoans. The strong liberal leanings of El Pasoans are demonstrated in the overwhelming electoral preference

for Democratic candidates over Republican candidates for many decades. Wilson's right-wing policy positions are of great concern to a
community that embraces equal treatment and opportunity for all.
Wilson was rated zero percent by the Human Rights Campaign for
her staunch opposition to LGBTQ rights and only 13 percent by the
ACLU because of her stance against civil rights legislation. She also
voted against funding for African American and Hispanic-serving
institutions. And she received an A rating from the National Rifle
Association (NRA).

Regarding her business dealings and influence peddling in
Washington, D.C., she has been called "the top illegal lobbyist"
for her consulting and billing practices on behalf of the Lockheed
subsidiary Sandia Corporation.[2] In 2007 the Committee on Responsibility and Ethics in Washington, D.C., or CREW, rated her among
the twenty-two most corrupt members of the U.S. Congress and, in
2017, CREW raised questions about her appointment as Secretary of
the Air Force. Also, during the George W. Bush administration Wilson
played a key role in the 2007 Karl Rove-engineered political hit job
against seven U.S. Attorneys, including David Iglesias of New Mexico.
The scandalous, Wilson-assisted dismissal of Iglesias, in addition to
the firing of the other U.S. Attorneys, unduly politicized the justice
system and caused disgust throughout the country.[3]

After the naming of Dr. Wilson as the sole UTEP finalist by the
Regents, the El Paso County Democratic Party passed a no-confidence
vote against her and the Texas Democratic Party asked that her name
be withdrawn from consideration, while Democratic legislators from
El Paso and elsewhere questioned her qualifications for the UTEP job
and criticized the search process. The Texas LGBTQ Legislative Cau-
cus, led by State Representative Mary González of El Paso, strongly
condemned Wilson's appointment, while El Paso State Senator José
Rodríguez characterized Dr. Wilson's appointment as "disrespectful of
UTEP students and faculty, as well as the community members who
reached out to the UT System at the beginning of the selection process." Added Rodríguez, "It [the appointment] also illustrates why this

*Virginia Martínez
and Dr. Tony
Kruszweski.
Courtesy anonymous
photographer.*

selection process, which provided very little campus or community engagement and produced only one finalist, is inherently flawed."[4]

As is to be expected, a segment of the community did back Dr. Wilson's selection. She had support among businesspersons and among politically conservative El Pasoans. The local Republican Party endorsed her appointment, as did seven hundred people who signed a CitizenGo.org petition created by the Binational Pro-Family

Pro-Life League of El Paso. Her biggest boosters in El Paso were Foster, Hunt, and Margo, with Foster and Margo making glowing statements about Wilson to the press upon her selection. To my knowledge, other members of the committee did not issue public statements.

Reaction to Wilson's Appointment among UTEP Faculty and Students

UTEP professors, administrators, staff, and students were even more stunned than community people when the news broke that Dr. Wilson had been named the sole finalist. A few faculty members expressed their outrage publicly, but most, afraid of repercussions, quietly shared their dismay with colleagues and friends. A survey conducted by the UTEP Faculty Senate revealed that 52.3 percent of the professoriate opposed Dr. Wilson's appointment, 27 percent supported it, and 20.7 percent did not express an opinion.

Among many of the students, the Wilson announcement hit like a ton of bricks. The news ignited a furious movement, especially among LGBTQ students, who knew about Dr. Wilson's homophobic views. Students and community sympathizers immediately launched a change.org petition that called for the Regents to withdraw her candidacy. Simultaneously, activists held loud demonstrations on and off campus. Students employed social media quite effectively, with an online group that had over 1,500 followers. In the UTEP Student Government Association annual elections, candidates' positions on the presidential appointee became a key issue. Eventually over ten thousand people signed the student led "UTEP Deserves Better" online petition, which read, in part:

> Wilson has a clear history of being anti-LGBTQ, as reflected in her voting record as a former U.S. congresswoman from New Mexico and more recently in her position as Air Force Secretary, where she reversed a rule to allow for anti-gay discrimination in 2018. For many students and staff, the university is a safe space to become and be freely who they are. Hiring someone that clearly does not reflect the ability to

Student protestors. Courtesy The Prospector.

support that for LGBTQ students is harmful. Moving Heather Wilson as the sole finalist, and potential next president of UTEP, endangers the university's ability to earnestly act on and serve in the best interests of all students.

Wilson attacked an anti-LGBT bullying bill, she voted in favor of a federal amendment to the U.S. Constitution that would ban marriage equality and voted against protections to the LGBT community. She also voted against a bill that would protect people in the workplace from being discriminated against based on their sexual orientation.

Other major concerns include Wilson's record of voting against the interests of students who depend on financial aid or loans to pay for their education. Records show she voted against lowering student loan interest rates and against providing year-round Pell grants (which is money the government provides to support students with financial need) and voted against millions of dollars that would have supported a new graduate Hispanic Serving Institution program.

UTEP deserves better. UTEP and the El Paso community deserve a president that reflects the university's values and the ability to serve and represent the best interest of all students.[5]

Conclusion

Based on the evidence regarding the presidential search process as well as recent political dynamics in El Paso, it is hard not to conclude that billionaire Paul Foster and other business persons, several with strong ties to the Republican Party, worked with the Republican top-heavy Board of Regents to carry out a political appointment. To many El Pasoans, especially Mexican Americans and UTEP students and faculty, Dr. Wilson was emphatically the wrong choice. She is a lightning rod, especially to LGBTQ people and civil rights advocates. She stirs controversy and division, lacks the academic qualifications and personal experience required to run a large border university, and her past business practices raise questions about ethics and conflicts of interest.

As El Paso's now (mid-2019) former representatives on the Board of Regents and prominent members of the search committee, Foster and Hunt could provide a valuable service by explaining what drove Dr. Wilson's appointment. As well, Mayor Margo, who is supposed to represent all El Pasoans, should disclose why he supported Dr. Wilson and not a better qualified candidate. Her selection continues to bewilder the community. Here are more questions to add to those posed in the introduction.

- Did the firm hired by the Regents to assist in the search vet Dr. Wilson properly? Did members of the search committee have complete information about her meager qualifications for the job, her problematic voting record on minority and LGBTQ issues, and her questionable ethics as a lobbyist and consultant? Word has leaked out that at least one member of the search committee knew little or nothing about this weighty negative baggage.

- Were there Latinos or Latinas among the candidates considered by the Regents? If so, why was one not chosen as a finalist?

- Why did the search committee and the Regents consider military and business experience, along with token higher education experience, of greater significance in choosing Dr. Wilson, than academic experience possessed by other candidates in positions such as university vice-president, provost, or president?

- What role did Dr. Wilson's connections with government agencies and lobbying background play in her selection? Did contract securement possibilities for local real estate companies, construction corporations, manufacturing firms, and other businesses enter into the decision-making process?

- Finally, was conservative ideology a reason for Dr. Wilson's appointment, given the expectation that she would respond favorably to possible offers from super-billionaires like David (now deceased) and Charles Koch to fund ultra-conservative or libertarian programs and institutes at UTEP? And/or to underwrite research and teaching projects of conservative faculty? And/or to encourage study groups among students who would be enticed by "Koch scholarships" to participate in discussions that emphasize why unregulated capitalism is good and government is bad? Foster in particular must have thought of the Koch-funded "academic" initiatives that have infiltrated numerous other universities. After all, Foster has had direct contact with the Koch brothers, attending at least one of their fund-raising events and meeting personally with Charles Koch. In 2014 Foster gave a million dollars to the Freedom Partners Action Fund, or FPAF, the Koch-sponsored Super PAC that is dedicated to electing right-wing politicians who advocate for such policies as slashing government regulations, cutting public social programs, and enacting voter suppression laws.[6]

VI. The Cheap, Disrespectful, and Contemptuous City Plan to Squeeze a Cultural Center into the Historic Downtown Library

OSCAR J. MARTÍNEZ[1]

In two city events held in September 2018, I witnessed firsthand what I had been hearing from many El Pasoans—that, with one or two exceptions, their city representatives and bureaucrats did not listen to citizens who dared point out defects in official policies or initiatives. A culture of "we know best" existed at city hall, and public concerns were routinely dismissed. Both events had to do with the mystifying merger plan adopted by the city regarding the downtown library/Mexican American Cultural Center project, and the furious community reaction to that proposal.

This is a story of a different aspect of "who rules El Paso," featuring the El Paso City Council and city staff. Bureaucrats dithered for several years regarding the setup for the Mexican American Cultural Center approved in the 2012 Quality of Life Bond, and eventually came up with a proposal that originated with a former head of the El Paso Library System that called for cramming the center into the Main Library. The city council approved the plan. There was no consideration of the physical impact of the center on the library,

El Paso Main Library. Photo by author.

the difficulties that tourists and residents would have reaching the facility in the crowded downtown area, nor any recognition of how substandard the center would be in comparison to kindred centers in other cities. Anyone on city staff who opposed the ill-conceived plan could not say so in public due to the "Code of Conduct" that requires all city employees to support official city positions.

This chapter presents a summary of the controversy, followed by personal statements and opinions expressed by numerous El Pasoans.

A Long-Awaited Mexican American Cultural and History Center

Dating back to at least the 1970s, there has been a desire in the Mexican American community in El Paso to have a center that celebrates Mexican American culture and history. After all, other cities with a Mexican American imprint had established such institutions, and it was only right that El Paso, with a predominantly Mexican American population and its long ties to Mexico should recognize and showcase its Mexican heritage. However, for decades the longing for a heritage center never went beyond the talking stage—with one exception: an immigration center proposed in the 1990s that unfortunately fell victim to growing concerns with border security and undocumented migration following the September 11, 2001, attacks in New York City.

Things changed in 2012 when El Paso voters approved a Quality of Life Bond ballot that, among other things, called for the creation of a Mexican American Cultural Center (MACC). It is important to point out that city officials apparently had given little thought to creating a cultural center prior to inserting it in the bond language and that it was likely added only to garner support for other preferred initiatives in Proposition 2. The initial allocation of $5.75 million for the cultural center out of the bond total of $243 million supports the claim that officials had given the center little consideration. The tactic of bundling several projects together in Proposition 2 worked for the city because by voting for Proposition 2, the voters expressed their support for the cultural center.

Mexican American Leaders Organize to Provide Input and Support for the Center

Knowing that the city had no concrete plans for the design and construction of the MACC, Mexican American leaders came together to form a new community organization, the Mexican American Cultural Institute (MACI), whose mission became to work with the city on the conceptualization, design, and building of the MACC. Prominent Mexican Americans, including elected officials, former city administrators, community leaders, attorneys, and businesspersons led the MACI effort, and hundreds of people attended MACI-sponsored meetings and made modest cash donations.

The City Rebukes MACI Efforts and All Other Community Input

As talks proceeded between the MACI leadership and the city in the years following the bond election, MACI sought representation on the MACC's Board of Directors and requested that the MACC be located in the Abraham Chávez Theatre. The two sides engaged in negotiations, but the discussions became complicated by changes in the composition of the city leadership following elections. In the end, city officials rejected the MACI proposals. Apparently, MACI board representation was out of the question because the city wanted to retain total control of the MACC. On the issue of where the MACC should be situated, the city ruled out the Abraham Chávez Theatre, claiming that renovating that venue would be too expensive. Another site would need to be found.

The city eventually broke relations with MACI over continuing differences of opinion and because the group did not meet the city's expectations regarding fundraising potential. MACI pointed out that fund raising could not be carried out because the city had refused to issue a Memorandum of Understanding (MOU) that formalized the participation of MACI in the project. Significant donations could not be secured without the MOU.

The city's dismissal of MACI and its go-it-alone policy raised serious concerns in the Mexican American community, especially after September 18, 2018, when the city council voted to place the MACC inside the west section of the Main Library. That meant taking away at least 40 percent of the library's space—space that ironically had been added to the library after the passage of a previous bond—and ending the possibility of the MACC having its own building. The idea of combining the MACC and the library had been previously discussed by a city-appointed committee, but practically nothing had been done to make the public aware of the plan.

When the word got out in the community that a second-rate

MACC was in the works, and that the downtown library would be significantly diminished, a firestorm broke out. Council representatives and city bureaucrats quickly learned that there was substantial opposition to their plan. A boisterous demonstration erupted on September 13 (five days before the council vote) at a city-sponsored show-and-tell event. I was among the protestors. On the day of the vote on September 18, twenty-five citizens, including myself, spoke out in council chambers against the plan. I and other MACC advocates demanded a first-class, stand-alone center, not a second-rate entity jammed into an existing building, while library supporters wanted the library to retain all its space and its programs left intact. With one exception, the council members ignored our pleas.

In the course of the protests, community activists questioned why the city kept hiring east-coast and European types unfamiliar with U.S. borderlands culture and history to oversee El Paso's cultural institutions. The Department of Museums and Cultural Affairs came under criticism for its failure to tap the expertise of local, PhD-level Mexican American historians who have decades of experience writing and lecturing about our border heritage. Protestors also wondered why the Hispanics on the city council did not support a top-of-the-line MACC. These representatives have displayed a lack of knowledge and appreciation for their own heritage, and they seem to be oblivious to the long-standing marginalization of Mexican Americans by the El Paso power structure.

In late 2018 and through 2019, the city's stubborn resolve to move forward with the library/cultural center merger plan provoked further indignation. For months opponents made their displeasure known through op-eds in local newspapers, petitions, posts on social media, and personal visits/emails/calls to the mayor and council representatives. On March 3, 2019, nearly one hundred persons attended a public forum to discuss whether the city's plan was a good or bad idea. The speakers included representatives from the city (Sam Rodríguez and Tracy Jerome), the library Friends, and MACI. The overwhelming sentiment among attendees was that the city's plan was a terrible idea. In a show of hands, only one person in the audience agreed with the city. Audience members urged city representatives to keep their hands off the library and to give the MACC its own stand-alone space.

In the aftermath of the August 3, 2019, Walmart massacre in our city, in which twenty-two people died and over two dozen were wounded at the hands of a white supremacist shooter who specifically targeted Mexicans/Mexican Americans, one of the speakers at a city council meeting suggested that the MACC plan should be redone with the aim of properly recognizing the many contributions of this group to El Paso. That could be accomplished by building a stand-alone, first-class MACC that would include a historical exhibit on discrimination and violence directed at Mexicans/Mexican Americans.

Lamentably, the city council representatives have not given any indication that they will chart a new course of action on the MACC. They have doggedly pressed on with their atrocious plan, issuing calls for bids regarding the design of the MACC-at-the-library configuration, even as widespread condemnation of the project persists. That disapproval from citizens is reflected in the selections that follow, which include abridged op-eds, letters, and emails written by concerned citizens, especially librarians.

The People Speak:
Pleas, Critiques, and Rebukes of the City Plan

Letter from Loida Garcia-Febo, President of the American Library Association, and Monique le Conge Ziesenhenne, PhD, President of the Public Library Association, to the mayor, members of the city council, city of El Paso, September 18, 2018.

We are writing to express our deep concern that the city of El Paso proposes to repurpose nearly half of the Main Library's physical space, displacing critical programs and support for children, teens, homeless residents, job seekers, and small business owners. As Presidents of the American Library Association and Public Library Association, representing thousands of librarians in Texas and across the country, we urge the city council to reject this proposal and ensure that both the Main Library and the Mexican American Cultural Center have adequate facilities to serve the community.

Public libraries are cornerstones of vibrant communities, providing access to educational, informational, cultural and recreational resources that strengthen the fabric of our democratic society. They are critical to a community's educational infrastructure, employment and business landscape, and social foundation. They are also a smart investment: in a 2017 study, the Bureau of Business Research at the University of Texas found that, for every dollar invested, public libraries yielded a return of $4.64 in economic benefits to their communities (link: https://www.tsl.texas.gov/roi).

While the economic benefit is important, the human impact of that investment is the real story. That impact is on view every day at Main Library—when a young patron discovers their first books and a path to literacy in the Children's Room; when a homeless resident is connected with vital social services; and when a job seeker is empowered with the guidance and resources to put their best foot forward and secure employment. El Paso's Main Library transforms the lives of residents every day and, in doing so, builds a stronger community.

El Pasoans made clear their desire for a Mexican American Cultural Center in a 2012 Quality of Life Bond vote. El Pasoans also declared their aspiration for a high-quality central library with passage of a Quality of Life Bond in 2000. One should not supplant the other, and it is unsurprising that key library and cultural center partners oppose a proposal that undermines both votes.

We are confident that the aspirations of the community can be realized with the preservation of the Main Library and development of a freestanding Mexican American Cultural Center. We ask you, therefore, to reject the current proposal and find a new site for the cultural center.

Marsha Labodda, comments before the El Paso City Council on September 18, 2018.

My name is Marsha Labodda. I am a taxpayer, voter, a retired school, public and academic librarian, member and presently President of the local Friends of Main Library, member of the Border Regional Library Association, the local chapter of REFORMA, an Association to Promote Library and Information Services to Latinos and the Spanish Speaking, and a member of Texas Library Association and the American Library Association.

We in the El Paso Library community were not consulted about the proposed renovation of Main Library by the Museum and Cultural Affairs Department that wants to take 40,000 square feet of their space for the Mexican Cultural Center/Institute as noted on the city's Public Release of September 11. The spaces that have been identified to be included in this renovation are the Children's Room, Teen Town, Literacy Center, Friends Bookstore, Employee Lounge, Circulation Work Room and Auditorium which was part of the 2000–2006 Bond Election expansion of the library. The Literacy Center recently inaugurated a three-year project with the Workforce Solution Borderplex last week. These spaces are now in jeopardy.

In 2000 we worked hard to get the bond project approved by the El Paso voters to expand their square footage to 100,000 square feet. This latest proposal will impact the services and place the library back to 2000. We should be moving forward, not backward.... We are in favor of having a cultural center hopefully with ample parking. Ben Fyffe was quoted as saying bus service is available, but I would argue that the bus service is not as reliable, fast or in all areas of El Paso. There is no rapid bus line in the West or East or Central areas. Parking downtown has been extremely limited and too costly for our lower or fixed income populations.

I have been in El Paso since 1976 and I am tired of the political intrigues, games, shenanigans, corruption and greed that I have witnessed over the years. We the voters and taxpayers voted you in with the trust that you would do the right thing for El Paso. But this proposal is not the right thing for El Paso nor the library. Keep it intact. We can come to a solution if all parties are included, not excluded and an agreement honestly and openly negotiated.

Katherine Brennand, "The MACC/Library Issue," El Paso Herald Post, September 21, 2018.

The leadership of my city broke my heart by approving the proposal to combine the Main Library and the Mexican American Cultural Center.

The majority of council members, except for Alexsandra Annello and Peter Svarzbein, expressed how they were going to vote on this issue BEFORE there was one single public comment. That is NOT what I call listening to one's constituents. Council reps doing that was shocking! [Note: In the end, only Alexsandra Annello voted against the proposal.]

At that juncture, we probably should have all walked out, chanting "What's the point?" But, hope springs eternal.

They had yet to hear letters written by presidents of both the National Library Association and the Texas Library Association, who were appalled that El Paso was doing this. They had yet to hear all the PhDs who spoke, or the artists, teachers and single moms, or the passionate librarians, whose life's work has been building that library!

A project had just been presented that will take over 40 percent to 45 percent of the Main Library, and the library folks were NOT even brought into the discussion until after the fact!....

...The city kept repeating there had been conversations, charrettes, public input and meetings about this over the past six years. That's true. I attended so many of them. However, a location for the cultural center at the Main Library was certainly never, ever presented....

How about a world class designed Mexican American Cultural Center, a beautiful and compelling tourist attraction, that would knock the socks off of any other heritage cultural center in the world?!....

...There was a masterful presentation about the upside; however, what about the downside? What kind of projected deficits will they run? How will the city deal with the emotional costs? The false perceptions? The disingenuousness? Losing the taxpayers' trust is a big price to pay.

Our population is 80 percent to 85 percent Mexican American, and we voted for a cultural center that would honor the heritage of the majority of our population....

...On September 18th, the die was cast before the vote was taken. Over one hundred people wasted at least three hours of their time. That's minimally three hundred hours of a most valuable commodity.

Jud Burgess, one of our most talented citizens, vehemently objected by saying: "This was a side show, a waste of time," and he got arrested.

So much for leadership!

The Undersigned Librarians, "El Paso Needs New Location for Cultural Center," El Paso Times, October 22, 2018.

We the citizens, voters and Friends of Main Library still have major reservations about the proposed repurposing of 40,000 square feet of the current Main Library to accommodate the MACC. The current Main Library...is a heavily-used cultural and community center for the development of life-long readers with nearly 200,000 users per year....

The continuing assurances from the Museum and Cultural Affairs Department (MCAD) that they will still seek more money from city council and the state because they know this project is underfunded does not give us any confidence that the repurposed Main Library will be fully restored in another section of the library. In addition, MCAD plans are grandiose but funding and space for the project seems to be lacking.

These plans were first revealed to the library community by the Bond Oversight Advisory Committee (BOAC) on September 10, 2018.... MCAD claimed they had presented these conceptual drawing plans to over two hundred focus groups and interviews from 2015 onward, yet the library community was left in the dark. Apparently, all were sworn to secrecy until after the city council's vote. There lies the lack of transparency.

We would like to work with the city of El Paso to create a successful project, and as concerned voters we will be continually monitoring the development of plans—in particular the repurposing of Main Library spaces....

Since this project has gone back and forth between MACI, MCAD, BOAC and the city for six years—waiting...will not hurt this project. How much money will MCAD get from state for this project?...

Libraries form the foundation of our culture, and a center such as the MACC will enhance it. We should preserve our Main Library that is so desperately needed in our community and find a suitable spot for the cultural center that our community deserves.

> Sharon Amastae, Oscar Baeza, Carol Brey,
> Jackie Dean, Marsha Labodda,
> Gretchen Trominski, Vona Van Cleef

Email from Margaret Neill to Oscar Martínez, June 18, 2019.

In my time as both the manager of the Main Library and the Co-Director of the El Paso Public Library System, I was never part of any discussions about the Mexican American Cultural Center taking over part of the Main Library building.

In the fall of 2018, as a private citizen, I attended a meeting with Ben Fyffe, who was discussing the MACC with library staff and friends of the library. He could offer no concrete information. He did not know how library services would be impacted, he did not know where library services would be re-located, he was unaware of who used the library or how they would be impacted. He repeatedly referred to a PowerPoint presentation that was also light on details, but heavy on architectural renderings and glossy depictions of smiling people walking around a newly constructed MACC.

As for the MACC, he spoke about a grab-bag of trendy ideas that had been floating around various government-centric magazines and blogs for a few years—a black box theater, a dance studio, a kitchen, a television studio, none of which had anything to do with Mexican American culture or heritage; when pressed about *how* those things would benefit a discussion of the history and culture of Mexican Americans, he was unable to articulate anything beyond how neat those things are. He also kept reiterating that those features would not be exclusively dedicated to Mexican American culture or history. He said that the city didn't want to "limit" the scope—which the group felt was strange, to say the least. Why install a kitchen if it's not to teach people about Mexican cooking? Why have a dance studio if it was not going to feature dances relevant to Mexican American culture? There are other organizations in El Paso, like Viva El Paso! or Cafe Mayapan that already do those things. Why re-invent the wheel?

In further meetings about the actual construction project, the city staff, including engineers, were unable to articulate how the old half of Main Library would be retrofitted to squeeze the expanded library back into its old, smaller space. They repeated the phrase "the space is underutilized" in lockstep but could not elaborate further. They were also unaware of the many, many facilities issues that Main Library has: electrical issues, flooding, flooring problems, elevator issues, etc., and I don't believe the modest budget they set for both retrofitting and "improving" a building that is over sixty years old will even begin to cover it, especially given the fact that the city does not have a preventative maintenance plan for its facilities and the Main Library has been suffering from benign neglect for decades.

All in all, it's disheartening to see this happening. I grew up at the downtown library and coming back, years later, to run it was one of my proudest moments. Leaving was hard.

Email from Marsha Labodda, President of the Friends of the Main Library, to the city representatives and mayor of El Paso, Texas, April 13, 2019.

During spring break, I had the opportunity to visit the Austin Mexican American Cultural Center and the Austin Public Library. I must say Austin's MACC is far better a site than the one proposed for here. It has 30,000 square feet with a potential to grow to 300,000 square feet and sits on 6½ acres. It has two separate buildings: an auditorium seating 212 and a two-story building with a gallery, classrooms, dance studio, library and Tejano genealogy computers area. All this came from a $20 million bond and is considered Phase I. Phase II will begin this year from a $27 million bond for storage and administration offices. Phase III will be sometime in the future.

What the Museum and Cultural Affairs Department of El Paso envisions is a far cry from Austin's MACC and I urge the city council and MCAD to delay this project until they can find more money and not take over the Main Library. Austin's Public Library is a separate building, six floors and a fantastic facility! It has the roof top garden, a café on the main street, a parking garage with one-hour free parking and auditorium on the first floor, which El Paso does not as its parking lot was turned into the Auditorium with the 2000 bond.

We deserve a great MACC but not at the expense of taking space from the Main Library. A better solution would be either get MACC its own building or expand the library the 47,000 square feet the MACC requires and tie it in with the history museum's space. Build a great MACC for our community, not a poorly funded and poorly designed one!

Email from Marshall Carter-Tripp to the mayor and council, February 12, 2019.

With regard to the cultural center that was voted on as part of a large package of projects in the 2012 Quality of Life Bond: It is indeed necessary that it be funded beyond the absurd original figure of $5.75 million. But the addition of $10.75 million is still not enough. If we examine the cultural centers in our nearest "competitor" city, Albuquerque, we find that more than twice the figure of $16.5 million was spent on the National Hispanic Cultural Center (NHCC) there. It is a stand-alone complex, with parking. Like the Indian Pueblo Center, it has dining options. I strongly suggest that you and members of council consider heading up to Albuquerque to take a look (link: http://www.nhccnm.org/).

What the city currently plans, shoehorning the center into the Main Library downtown, will be a disaster, and I'd guess in the tourist business it will be a laughing-stock. For the Hispanic citizens of El Paso it's more of a slap in the face. And for those of us who value libraries, the same. The combined library-cultural center will eliminate a large chunk of the remaining green space downtown. It will have no parking, so please imagine how visitors and residents on a baseball weekend will get to the center? Not to mention how it will be affected by the numerous festivals that close off downtown. And it will hardly be large enough to contain all the exhibits and activities that a really first-class center would include.

If the city is determined to put the cultural center downtown, why not consider the now-empty building of the former Exploreum, which is close to the convention center and has substantial parking available. Or use one of the architectural treasures scattered around downtown. Be creative! Make El Paso proud!!

Op-ed by Carmen Rodríguez and Oscar J. Martínez, "El Paso City Council, don't ruin Main Library for Mexican American Cultural Center," El Paso Times, February 25, 2019.

This is to make it known, especially to local government leaders, that there is very strong opposition in the community to the city's plan to take away 40 percent of the downtown public library in order to make room for the Mexican American Cultural Center (MACC). We have heard such opposition over the last several months during petition drives, in public forums, and as part of our involvement in the creation of Community First, a new coalition of local organizations, leaders, and activists.

It is felt that the implementation of the city's plan will seriously damage the library, an institution that El Pasoans love and want to keep whole....

...And what about the MACC? We have no doubt that, once informed of the facts, El Pasoans would overwhelmingly support the cultural center having its own building. Certainly a "signature" project for the city deserves as much. The truth is that the city had little interest in a cultural center and embraced it only to gain support for passage of the bond in 2012. It is important to remember that in 2000 the voters supported a Quality of Life Bond that provided for the improvement and expansion of the library. But now a slate of new city representatives has no problem diminishing the library and undoing what voters supported in the past. Where is the fairness in that?

If the city is not willing to do justice to the MACC, it should at least drop its plans to shove it into the library. The members of the Mexican American Cultural Institute (MACI), who worked for years conceptualizing the cultural center, have come to the same conclusion.

They see preservation of the Main Library as a top priority as well and would rather continue working for a stand-alone cultural center that is first class and will bring pride to the city.

Op-ed by Kathy Staudt and Verónica Frescas, "El Paso Public Library basement is no place for books," El Paso Times, April 5, 2019.

Our main downtown library is precious space. That space is being cut by 40 percent to make room for a Mexican American Cultural Center. City bureaucrats decided to put both the existing book collection and literacy center in the "first sub-basement" of the building. The relocation downward constitutes nearly 17,000 square feet of library space according to city figures at their March 3rd presentation. City council representatives approved this plan last fall perhaps without bothering to read the details. The city's plan raises more questions than it answers.

Our city council government is relying on our community to forget what was actually voted on the 2012 Quality of Life Bond: to *improve* the main downtown library facility and to have a stand-alone Hispanic Cultural Heritage Center, not squeeze one into the other.

We propose to delay the city's effort to slash library space and move the city's largest collection into the claustrophobic basement. Will materials in the basement now—reference, periodicals, books in Spanish, and government documents—go even deeper to the second sub-basement? What about restrooms? The dingy basement has only two single-use bathrooms for the public. If more people visit a multi-use facility, where will they park: in the $10-per-car lots? What about the asbestos from the last renovation round: how much more remediation is needed, at what cost? We could go on and on.

The project to carve up the library is not technically feasible. It exemplifies the city's approach to economic development: tear down structures, rebuild them, and celebrate costly temporary job creation, all at taxpayers' expense. Instead, we say delay the project and start interacting with diverse constituencies in the community rather than presenting them with a *fait accompli*.

The downtown library draws about 200,000 users annually. Let's double those figures! El Paso should celebrate literacy and reading, not diminish them by scrunching materials into the basements. A fraction of library users has no access to computers and technology. Will they be turned away, as they are from downtown museums?

On March 3rd, the El Paso Social Justice Forum hosted a panel discussion about the downtown library and Mexican American Cultural Center. For the almost hundred people, outrage broke out when hearing comments by Friends of the Library representatives, the Mexican American Cultural Institute representative, Sam Rodríguez, the city engineer, and the director of this plan, Ms. Tracy Jerome. Some audience members raised questions like "How do we stop this likely train wreck?" In no uncertain terms, we asked Ms. Jerome to communicate to the city our deep dismay over their plans. Yet in a recent presentation to city council, she listed the Social Justice Forum as one among many examples of "community engagement." What a travesty!

The renovation plans made behind closed doors, then listed as community engagement, underline the ugly alienation and lack of transparency that has developed between El Pasoans and their city council. Instead, representatives seem to listen mainly to those who make large contributions during election campaigns. We in the Community First Coalition share frustration and anger about the way the city is managed and controlled. We want to live in and contribute to a city that maintains its authenticity and soul. The move to squeeze books into the library basement is but one of many examples of this race to the bottom of representative government.

VII. The Ongoing Saga of the "Lost Dog Trail"[1]

THE COLLECTIVE

On May 4, 2019, the voters of El Paso, in their first-ever opportunity to save a specific area of natural open space from development, voted overwhelmingly—by over 88 percent—to save 1,107 acres of land, popularly known as the "Lost Dog Trail,"[2] as natural open space in perpetuity. This remarkable vote came on the heels of the 2018 city of El Paso's designation of that land, located in the west side of the city, as a Tax Increment Reinvestment Zone (TIRZ) Number 12 in order to promote its development in this sprawling city.

This essay provides background and context to understand open space, smart growth, and city measures to—ironically—both protect natural space through citizen action and undermine it by fostering development through city bureaucratic means like the TIRZ concept, about which the general public knows little. This overview essay of dense and complex land and power issues illustrates the importance of civil society oversight and pushback through non-government/nonprofit organizations, city board appointments, social mobilization, petition drives, and voter-turnout efforts.

The lesson of Lost Dog is that El Pasoans can renew democracy in land use policies with creative, persistent, and intense civic action. Most importantly, constant vigilance is necessary given continuous threats from developers and official government bodies.

The Rise of Non-Governmental/Nonprofit Organizations: Civic Action

In the 1970s, following city efforts to carry out development projects on the Franklin Mountains, strong pushback came from the quickly formed Franklin Mountains Wilderness Coalition. As a result, by 1987, the state government had acquired over 24,000 acres on the mountain and opened the Franklin Mountains State Park, the largest urban park in the nation.

A decade later, new efforts to reduce sprawl and institute "smart growth" principles got underway, along with efforts focused on identifying and protecting existing open space and projecting future open space acquisition. An Open Space Master Plan was approved by the city in early 2007. Several self-identified "progressives" on city council worked with staff for two years to create Plan El Paso, implementing the principles of "smart growth"; this plan won several awards after its adoption in 2012. However, the Open Space Master Plan has been mostly dormant. At the time of its creation, only about 1 percent of the land area of the city, not quite 2,000 acres, had been designated as open space (excluding the Franklin Mountains State Park), a sad comparison to neighboring cities such as Albuquerque, with some 30,000 acres of city-owned open space.

For many years hikers and bikers used the Lost Dog area for recreation. The number of people who enjoyed this land increased as its desirability spread among outdoor enthusiasts, even as surrounding tracts morphed into residential communities. In 2011, members of the Borderland Mountain Bike Association (BMBA), a nonprofit organization, finalized a lease of the area with the Public Service Board (PSB) and the El Paso Water Utilities (EPW) that allowed for the creation of a trailhead and trails for biking and hiking. Using its own funds and labor, BMBA maintained this area as a free and accessible natural open space for low-impact recreation.

Over the years, city officials, the PSB, and the EPW made plans for Lost Dog and surrounding space. With parallel but alternative visions about that space, government bodies and developers had their eyes on the Lost Dog area as far back as 2005, with an official plan produced in 2013 to foster a residential and commercial community complete with roads and utilities.[3]

The First Citizen Petition, 2015

Concerned over development of open space on both sides of the Franklins, in 2015 local citizens initiated a "We the People" online petition, calling for preservation in perpetuity of over 8,000 acres of city-owned undeveloped natural land. As a result of the 3,116 signatures to this petition, EPW worked with the open space supporters to create a Preservation and Conservation Planning Committee/Group to study how much of the open space could be preserved and how much would be appropriate for development. The group was made up of city staff, open space advocates, and development advocates. After meeting for two years, in August 2017 they produced the report, "Enrich, Enhance and Elevate El Paso, Texas: Recommendations to Establish Criteria for the Preservation of Public Land in El Paso." It was presented to the PSB on March 18, 2018, but the Lost Dog trail area was not included in this plan.

Official Motivations and Tools to Develop Lost Dog

Among their responsibilities for providing water, sewage and storm-water services for El Pasoans, the PSB and EPW are also responsible for planning for the city's future water supply. With the cost of water increasing due to depletion of the Hueco Bolson aquifer, the solutions that PSB/EPW have developed include advanced water purification, water reuse, desalination, conservation and, in the long term, piped-in water from aquifers in Hudspeth and Culbertson Counties. Several of these are expensive. PSB/EPW, which did not want to raise water rates but rather to generate more funds, decided to start selling public land, including thousands of acres around the Franklin Mountains.

On December 13, 2017, the PSB declared the land known as Lost Dog "inexpedient" to their system. This was the first step in transferring the land to the city of El Paso, a move that made it available for development under the Transmountain Corridor and Northwest Regulating Plan. On February 14, 2018, the PSB initiated a two-year, $250,000 agreement with the Borderplex Alliance (which morphed out of the Paso del Norte Group; see Section I) to identify "potential buyers and lessees for EPW-owned property" and to "maximize...the use of land owned and/or controlled by PSB/EPW." This plan was expected to "return significant monetary benefits to the Utility [EPW], its ratepayers, and the citizens of the El Paso region."[4]

On May 29, 2018, the city approved the creation of TIRZ 12 on the Lost Dog property, an action that provided for the selection of a "master developer" and development of the area. The TIRZ 12 encompasses some 1,107 acres abutting the west side of the Franklin Mountains State Park. This PSB-controlled area, which includes some heavily used hiking and biking sites, ensures long-term water supplies without raising rates as noted above. City council voted in May 2018 to entice development here by investing part of the resulting property taxes in infrastructure under the provisions of a TIRZ. The land would be sold to an un-named private entity for the construction of nearly 10,000 housing units and over 800,000 square feet of commercial space. Massive public outcry resulted in a petition to block this project, but the council rejected the petition.[5]

Environmentalists continued the rescue effort by taking the issue to the citizenry. On July 17, 2018, the first set of petitions to preserve Lost Dog from development by terminating TIRZ 12 was validated by the city clerk, with 1,834 signatures verified, well over the minimum of 1,666. The signatures were gathered in only two weeks. After the approval of the Save Lost Dog petition to put the issue on the ballot, leaders of the effort met with the city suggesting a compromise. The city rejected their overture and told them they would lose the election.[6]

From Petition to Ballot:
The People's Overwhelming Vote Success

On September 12, 2018, a second set of petitions was validated with 1,977 signatures (minimum required: 1,666). After the success of the second petition, the city, in its October 30 meeting, put additional covenants on the Lost Dog land through water and sewer bonds in an attempt to block the citizens' campaign. This was futile because the PSB had already declared the land inexpedient. In dealing with city hall, Lost Dog leaders encountered officials who were disrespectful and heavy-handed. It seemed clear that the city leadership was out of touch with the people.[7]

On May 4, 2019, the voters were asked to approve or reject preservation in perpetuity of the Lost Dog land in its natural state. In a record-shattering election, over 88 percent of the voters voted to save Lost Dog. This was the first time, as far as is known, that the citizens of El Paso successfully used the petition process and passed a proposition meant to provide natural open space that serves the common good. Before that, scores of environmentalists had made proposals in many public meetings to no avail.

How did this unprecedented success happen? A loose network of people met every few weeks, planned the effort to save Lost Dog and fanned out into the community spreading the word. Some people collected signatures at biking, hiking and other public events; others went door to door in neighborhoods throughout the city; others phoned those who had signed petitions; emails were sent to environmental groups to encourage them to explain the effort to their members and to spread the word; and many folks simply talked to their friends and neighbors. Many individuals carried petitions with them wherever they went. Volunteers wore t-shirts and carried signs to increase Lost Dog visibility. They also handed out large information cards. In addition, Lost Dog advocates wrote letters to the editor and opinion columns in local newspapers and used social media.

As the election approached, a campaign committee was formed, and fund-raising took place. Funding allowed ads to be placed on local TV stations and other media. Media outlets regularly carried news stories that alerted many people to the issue. Those who gathered signatures met people of all ages and backgrounds. It was gratifying to see the overwhelming support of the vast majority of people contacted. All of these many efforts led to success.

The City Reacts

Prior to the election, the city attempted, through "press releases" and social media postings, to assure citizens that much of the TIRZ 12 would be preserved as open space, and to warn that over $11 million would be owed by the city to the PSB if the voters approved the Lost Dog proposition. Voters did not buy the city's arguments. After the election, the city council had no choice but to pass an ordinance to formalize the preservation of Lost Dog.

On July 17, 2019, city staff made a presentation to the City Open Space Advisory Board (OSAB) asking for their advice on five options for compensating the PSB for the Lost Dog land that could no longer be sold. OSAB decided that the Lost Dog land should be 1) re-zoned as natural open space, 2) that TIRZ 12 on the Lost Dog land should be rescinded, and 3) that the city should pursue placing a conservation easement on the Lost Dog land and allow it to remain in the PSB inventory.

City staff took the OSAB recommendations into account as they prepared a report for the city council, which the staff presented at a meeting on July 23, 2019. The report provided an analysis of preservation costs, funding concerns, and preservation options for the Lost Dog area. Members of the public opposed the city staff recommendations, instead proposing a conservation easement, natural open space zoning, and dissolution of TIRZ 12. Following discussion in executive session, council members voted to get more information about conservation easements and determination of the fair market value of the land to be paid to PSB over a five- to ten-year period. The wording of the motion called for city staff to develop proposals, including the dissolution of the TRIZ 12, in the next ninety days. One of the issues was whether to leave the Lost Dog land in the EPW inventory for dual purpose use as a natural storm-water management system and a natural open space amenity.

The ninety-day postponement mandated on July 23 was in addition to the May 2019 ninety-day postponement (the "stakeholder phase") to determine preservation methods, costs and optimal funding sources. At this writing (August 26, 2019), the Lost Dog saga continues with those major issues unresolved. This means despite the people's vote, the future of the Lost Dog land is not yet certain.

Proposed Great Wolf Land Swap

Another ongoing land issue is the city manager's initiative to have the Great Wolf Lodge company build a resort in El Paso, despite the lack of any published evidence that this would bring significant economic benefits to El Paso (and no quality-of-life benefits for residents, as only hotel guests can use the indoor water park). In order to entice the company to build the resort, the council and mayor approved a plan to acquire forty-four acres of land as the site for the project from Paul Foster's FSW Company. In exchange for the forty-four acres, which are located next to Interstate-10 on the west side of the city, Foster's company would receive 2,313 acres of city-owned undeveloped land on the northeast side of the city. The city maintains that the assessed value of the privately-owned forty-four acres, $18.6 million, is the same as the value of city-owned 2,313 acres, also $18.6 million. That is hard to believe. Great Wolf Lodge would be able to acquire the forty-four acres for $20,000, which speaks volumes about the politics of land in El Paso. The county commissioners also approved tax breaks for the company. Great Wolf has until mid-2020 to decide if it will take the deal.[8]

Opponents of the deal with the Great Wolf Lodge pointed out the absence of transparency and lack of concern for public input on the part of city officials. Doug Schwartz, CEO at Southwest Land Development, asked the city council to postpone deciding for a month so that the public could become better informed. "First let me say that we want to see the Great Wolf Lodge locate in El Paso," Schwartz wrote. "What we do not want to see is the city and the taxpayers get fleeced just to make a deal. With the terms that have been made public, it is apparent that the city is giving away the farm to Great Wolf Lodge and FSW Investments."[9]

Strategies for the Future of Open Space:
Constant Vigilant Action is Necessary

As the Lost Dog story illustrates, the most important strategy for citizens to achieve preservation of natural open space is through consistent and persistent advocacy to the city council, city advisory boards, city staff, and the PSB/EPW. Environmentalists need to be knowledgeable about the extraordinarily complex planning documents buried in official websites, meeting agendas, and minutes. This strategy has been used with some success. Consider two recent examples involving city land purchases for open space. After civic activism, it took three years to achieve positive results in the case of Knapp Canyon, a 366-acre area on the slopes of the Franklin Mountains in Northeast El Paso, and twenty years in the case of Kern View Estates II (with help from former council member Ann Morgan Lilly and the Mission Hills Neighborhood Association.)

Those who believe in the innate value of natural open space, those who enjoy getting out into natural open space for recreation, those who appreciate the views of the Franklin Mountains, and those who feel that the Franklins are fundamental to the identity of their city all have a passion for preservation of the land. Lost Dog voters in May 2019 shared a common sentiment that there is enough development in El Paso. The loss of natural open space that people can see and feel as a tangible experience of El Paso life stimulated a deep upwelling of support for the Lost Dog trails area. Both the widespread support and the significant raw numbers of the positive vote are a way of telling our elected officials "PLEASE, WE WANT MORE NATURAL SPACE!"

Builders and their suppliers have benefited from the continuing development sprawl, particularly from mountainside development. Their massive support for like-minded council members (see section III, questioning El Paso's "pay-to-play" system) poses constant challenges to smart growth.

Successful civic victories take time, persistence, money, petitions, and organized volunteer mobilization. While open-space advocates serve on boards and commissions, those individuals can hardly make a difference unless the city council and other public bodies push the natural open space agenda, with a simultaneous push by city civic advocates. Land preservation must be made a priority. The public can and should bring up the issue during electoral campaigns. To assure the electoral victory of council members who truly represent the people, not simply developers' interests, large numbers of people need to vote and use civic tools and numerical power to push candidates and their representatives to do the right thing. Some land preservation advocates should consider a run for office as well!

Conclusion

THE COLLECTIVE

This book has presented troubling analyses of the poor state of local democracy in the city of El Paso. But we also offer a ray of hope.

In recent years, a handful of very wealthy, primarily non-Spanish surnamed people, have manipulated and controlled an agenda to put the city in heavy debt with so-called Quality of Life Bonds. The 2012 bond election is a prime example. It offered voters three deliberately vague issues about which to affirm support so that politicians and city-hall bureaucrats could move forward with lots of discretionary cash. El Pasoans have seen delays, cost overruns, and a mounting indebtedness that our stagnant-sized population will hardly be able to handle in five to ten years.

While the baseball stadium boondoggle may already be a done deal, the land grab of the historic neighborhood Duranguito is not. Through energetic defense of the neighborhood, expertise, and legal strategies, the project has been stalled. And in the delay, larger numbers of El Pasoans and allies for Duranguito defenders have grown, using other rationales—largely the fiscal irresponsibility of city management and politicians who are beholden to developers who will reap profits with construction and building at the start of new projects, then take their money and run, saddling El Pasoans with more debt.

Indeed, in 2019, city politicians successfully pushed a near-half-billion dollar bond to cover the basics: deferred maintenance, police department staffing, and the like. It is nothing short of manipulative attempts to appease voters with a "choice" like this. The city's basic functions should not be a choice.

Besides the big-money bond debts, El Pasoans are left with pathetic efforts in the city's so-called "quality-of-life" initiatives. These include a proposed squeezed-in Mexican American Cultural Center (MACC) in the downtown library, with the prospect that El Paso will get a second-rate center and the library will be diminished. Books will be dumped in the library's basement and sub-basements. City representatives have given little thought to parking problems for those facilities, ignoring the disappearing low-cost street parking and seemingly oblivious to the profiteering at recently constructed parking lots that charge high fees that we know deter visitors to the downtown area.

The length of our contributions in this book surpass those of newspaper articles in our major media sources: the daily *El Paso Times* and *Diario de El Paso*, and the weekly business-oriented paper, *El Paso Inc.* Print newspapers have shrunk in subscribership not only in El Paso, but nationwide, due in part to ruthless cost-cutting by national owners. The digital versions are scanty and not user-friendly. However, we must support journalists' oversight—preferably expanded oversight—if we are to restore some semblance of democracy to El Paso city government. Even a business weekly can reveal division with the business class, for good business practice seeks fair competition, not publicly subsidized business in a "pay-to-play" system. For example, a mid-July 2019 *El Paso Inc.* article titled "Study Scrutinizes El Paso Electric Sale" features critical questions raised by former mayor Larry Francis and businessman Ted Houghton regarding who the real beneficiaries will be of the El Paso Electric Company recent sale—investors or customers? We doubt it is or will be the customers.

Dealing with the massive amount of money spent on local elections by the folks who have the big bucks appears to be the most daunting issue in El Paso. Other cities, such as Austin, have passed ordinances limiting the amounts individuals can contribute. Reform advocates in El Paso can certainly give campaign contribution limits a try by working to place the issue on an election ballot. In the short run, reformers can put candidates on the spot by asking them to pledge to only accept modest contributions from donors, perhaps no more than $400 from any contributor. Those who do not accept the pledge would be called out publicly for all voters to see. Social media can be a great help here.

The low turnout in El Paso elections complicates reform efforts. Advocates who want to get the most progressive candidates elected need to concentrate their efforts on registering new voters while conducting voter education sessions regarding who is running for office, what propositions appear on the ballot, and who is behind them. This calls for more sustained activity on the part of citizen volunteers.

In a city where Mexican Americans (83 percent of the population) continue to lack the capacity to elect enough representatives who truly promote their interests and where the group is unable to stop undesirable initiatives by developers and city officials, it is important to address the major causes of such powerlessness. The fact that most Mexican-descent people in El Paso occupy a low economic status undeniably plays a large role in voting behavior and other forms of civic participation. But the ideology of those in positions of influence and power, disproportionately white European Americans, must also be considered.

Two examples are illustrative. First, what has driven economic elites and public decision makers to want to destroy Duranguito in order to make room for an arena, instead of recognizing that neighborhood as El Paso's birthplace and appreciating the value of transforming it into a historical district that celebrates our indigenous and Mexican heritage? Why are the poor and oldest Mexican American neighborhoods not given the same consideration for historic designation as other neighborhoods? Historical districts can be of great educational benefit for all El Pasoans and a great boost for tourism. Why not embrace this latter option?

Second, what drove local economic elites to engineer the selection of Dr. Heather Wilson as UTEP president, knowing full well that she had weak academic credentials, a highly problematic record as a politician and business consultant, and zero experience to lead a large, Hispanic-serving institution on the border? Why did the Paul Foster/Woody Hunt/Mayor Dee Margo-led search committee refuse to add at-large Mexican American community representatives to that body? Most significantly, why was a Latina or Latino not seriously considered for the position? After all, Mexican Americans have been waiting for over a century to have one of their own preside over UTEP, whose student body is now over 80 percent Hispanic.

In both the Duranguito and UTEP cases, to some extent economic and political interests explain the overt actions by those in control of the decision-making process. But what about the more subtle roles played by race, ethnicity, and class regarding these and other issues? Historical evidence demonstrates that numerous policies and actions of the power elite in El Paso in past decades were shaped by 1) expediency, ignorance, indifference, or insensitivity to Mexican American concerns, as well as by 2) unvarnished anti-Mexican sentiment.[1] We know that discrimination, prejudice and classism persist amongst us. The way they are manifested in modern times has been indirect and mostly imperceptible. In fact, the way El Pasoans deal with racism is exactly the way we have addressed it, or rather alluded to it, in this book.

To illustrate, we have indeed called attention to ethnic/racial and class characteristics of powerful individuals and groups involved in decision-making, e.g. "mostly white economic elites," "elitists out of touch with the mainstream community," "white, wealthy donors with access to power," "unqualified to lead a large Hispanic-serving university," "dismissal of requests from Mexican American leaders," "not Spanish-speaking," "paltry acquaintance with Mexican heritage, history and culture," "long-standing marginalization of Mexican Americans by the El Paso power structure," "glaringly racist and elitist imagery," "displacement of low-income immigrants," "defense of Mexican American barrios...."

In making these points, however, we have not alleged racism; we have not labeled intentions, actions, or policies as being racist. We are cognizant that charging racism is a serious matter. And we know that documenting or proving racist intent is extremely difficult because power brokers, or any decision-makers for that matter, seldom reveal their motives outside their exclusive circles.

We are aware that well-placed Mexican Americans with a deferential or self-interest mentality often do the bidding of the power elite while going against the interests of their own people. Moreover, this situation is made more complex by wealthy Mexicans from Ciudad Juárez with business interests in El Paso forsaking their identity as they carry on alliances with rich folks north of the Rio Grande.

Regardless of how decisions have originated regarding multiple issues in El Paso, we cannot ignore the fact that many of them have had racist outcomes. What most of us can agree on is that institutional racism, systemic racism and elitism are alive and well in El Paso. Perhaps it is more difficult or impossible for the powerful and the privileged to understand, let alone acknowledge it. Because of this, those of us who put our community first have a responsibility to be alert and call it out when we perceive it.

On a more positive note, the ray of hope in this book comes from activists who engineered the spectacularly successful Lost Dog Trail election victory in May 2019. Those volunteers demonstrated how El Pasoans, if enthusiastic and mobilized in civil society action, can reverse the agendas and profiteering of the political-economic elite and their handmaidens in city hall bureaucracy. The story of the Lost Dog vote, in which virtually every part of the city came out to vote for open space and trail preservation against the strenuous efforts of city staff and council to ensure that the proposition did not pass and development could proceed on the mountainside, is a strong signal that we can indeed fix what is wrong. It may not be easy but, with sustained effort, El Pasoans can take back their city.

Postscript: Lessons from the Walmart Massacre

THE COLLECTIVE

On August 3, 2019, as we were putting the finishing touches on this book, an unprecedented, racially motivated massacre occurred in El Paso that shocked us to our core. Never in our lifetimes had bigotry and hate raised its ugly head against our Mexican American population in such an extreme, bold-faced, and cold-blooded manner. A white supremacist from north Texas travelled over six hundred miles to our city seeking to kill people of Mexican heritage. As revealed in his "manifesto," his aim was to stop an ongoing "invasion" of Texas by undesirable immigrants. He opened fire with an assault weapon on shoppers at a Walmart store, killing twenty-two people and wounding over two dozen others.

This horrific event is the latest of numerous recent mass shootings that have occurred in the United States. These attacks have been linked to racial hatred and have been facilitated by extremely weak gun control laws. White nationalists who abhor the growing ethnic and racial diversity in our society have increasingly turned to violence to prevent the United States from becoming a "non-white" majority country. The mestizo Mexican/Mexican American population is seen as one of the major groups that is threatening the numerical supremacy of white European Americans. That is the national context for understanding what happened in our city.

How is the Walmart tragedy related to the issues discussed in this book? Simply put, concern over the safety of El Pasoans dwarfs all the issues that we have discussed. The vulnerability of all our people, especially the Hispanic population, has been exposed. Well-armed domestic terrorists can strike anywhere at any moment.

For decades, government bodies at all levels have done little to enact effective gun control laws. It is shameful that in the aftermath of the Walmart massacre, the mayor of El Paso, the Texas governor, and the two U.S. senators from Texas meticulously avoided talking about gun control, instead following the old Republican playbook of sending "thoughts and prayers" to victims and calling for the creation of commissions to study the roots of such problems as mental illness, racism, and white supremacy, charging such bodies to make recommendations on how to diminish these societal maladies. These actions have been proven to be nothing more than delay and avoidance tactics. Fortunately, some of our leaders in El Paso have forcefully emphasized the need to pass gun control legislation, most notably State Senator José Rodríguez, congresswoman Verónica Escobar and presidential candidate Beto O'Rourke, all Democrats.

Tragically, the rhetoric of the Walmart shooter matched some of the words that came from the 2015–16 Donald Trump presidential campaign and the White House thereafter. Hateful language has also emanated from the Texas governor's mansion. For example, in a fund-raising appeal dated the day before the El Paso attack, Governor Greg Abbott admonished supporters to "defend" the state against "illegal immigrants"…, "drug traffickers, and violent gangs [that] swarm our border." The governor decried the "crisis at the southern border" and called for "taking matters into our own hands."

It is well known that the Republican party has blocked gun control legislation for many years. Alas, some of the local economic elite donors' names documented in Section III can be found on websites that show huge sums donated to the dominant party in power at the state and national levels—sums that range from a half-million to a million dollars in 2014 and 2018. Readers should visit neutral websites with information about campaign contributions, such as the Federal Elections Commission (www.fec.gov) and Open Secrets (www.opensecrets.org). Donors probably also contribute through "dark money" sites—not publicly available information. The large sums help to perpetuate laws that allow military-style semi-automatic and automatic assault weapons—like those used in the El Paso massacre—to be sold and used in civil society. The weapons are designed to kill, and kill quickly, in war. They have no place in our streets, our schools, our churches, our synagogues, our mosques, our malls, our stores, our recreational spaces, etc.

One would expect that folks in our community who are inclined to donate money to a political party would withhold such support if that organization cares more about maintaining power than keeping people safe. We have a right to expect this from our fellow citizens because this issue has become a matter of life and death. All El Pasoans, from the marginalized to the privileged, must do their part to make sure our city is made secure for everyone.

Appendix

CITY OF EL PASO, TEXAS
ELECTED OFFICIALS AND ADMINISTRATIVE OFFICERS,
2005–2021

66th Election (May 7, 2005)
Term 2005–2007 & 2005–2009
(staged terms to switch to four-year terms)

John F. Cook, (2005–2009) First Term Mayor
Ann Morgan Lilly, (2005–2007) District 1 (West)
Susie Byrd, (2005–2009) District 2 (West Central)
*José Alexandro Lozano, (2005–2009) District 3 (East Central)
Melina Castro, (2005–2009) District 4 (Northeast)
Presi Ortega, Jr., (2005–2007) District 5 (East)
Eddie Holguín, Jr., (2005–2007) District 6 (East-Lower Valley)
Steve Ortega, (2005–2009) District 7 (Lower Valley)
Beto O'Rourke, (2005–2007) District 8 (South-West)
Richarda Duffy Momsen, City Clerk
Joyce A. Wilson, September 7, 2004, City Manager
*Submitted his resignation on Tuesday, January 2, 2008, to run for another office.
Emma Acosta was elected to fulfill the term

67th Election (May 12, 2007)
Term 2007–2011

Ann Morgan Lilly, District 1 (West)
Rachel Quintana, District 5 (East)
Eddie Holguín, Jr., District 6 (East-Lower Valley)
Beto O'Rourke, District 8 (South-West)
Richarda Duffy Momsen, City Clerk
Joyce A. Wilson, City Manager

Special Election (May 10, 2008)
Term 2008–2009

Emma Acosta, District 3 (East Central)

68th Election (May 9, 2009)
Term 2009–2013

John F. Cook, Second Term Mayor
Susie Byrd, District 2 (West Central)
Emma Acosta, First Term District 3 (East)
Carl Robinson, District 4 (Northeast)
Steve Ortega, District 7 (Lower Valley)
Richarda Duffy Momsen, City Clerk
Joyce A. Wilson, City Manager

69th Election (May 14, 2011)
Term 2011–2015

Ann Morgan Lilly, Second Term District 1 (West)
Dr. Michiel R. Noe, First Term District 5 (East)
Eddie Holguín, Jr., District 6 (East-Lower Valley)
Cortney Carlisle Niland, First Term District 8 (South-West)
Richarda Duffy Momsen, City Clerk
Joyce A. Wilson through June 10, 2014, City Manager

70th Election (May 11, 2013)
Term 2013–2017

Oscar Leeser, First Term, sworn in on June 24, 2013, Mayor (Number 49)
Larry Romero, First Term District 2 (West Central)
Emma Acosta, Second Term District 3 (East)
Carl L. Robinson, Second Term District 4 (Northeast)
Lilia (Lily) Limón, First Term District 7 (Lower Valley)
Richarda Duffy Momsen, City Clerk
Tomás González, June 24, 2014, City Manager

Special Election District 6 (July 19, 2014)
Term 2014–2015

Claudia Ordaz, District 6 (East-Lower Valley)
Note: Claudia Ordaz to fill remainder of Eddie Holguin, Jr.'s Term. Mr. Holguín
  resigned to run for another position/office with El Paso County.

71st Election (May 9, 2015)
Term 2015–2019

Runoff: Peter Svarzbein and Al Weisenberger, District 1 (West)
Dr. Michiel R. Noe, Second Term District 5 (East)
Claudia Ordaz, First Term District 6 (East-Lower Valley)
Cortney Carlisle Niland, Second Term District 8 (South-West)
Richarda Duffy Momsen, City Clerk
Tomas González, City Manager

Special Runoff Election for District 1 (June 19, 2015)

Peter Svarzbein, First Term District 1 (West)
Larry Romero, District 2, Resignation Letter submitted February 11, 2016,
  effective February 23, 2016, due to illness.

Special Election for District 2 (May 7, 2016)

Jim Tolbert elected for District 2, to fill an unexpired term left vacant by
  Representative Larry Romero. Representative Jim Tolbert was sworn in
  on May 17, 2016. Term began May 17, 2016, and expired 2017.
Jim Tolbert, Filling an Unexpired Term, District 2 (West Central)

72nd Election (May 6, 2017)
Term 2017–2021

Dee Margo, First Term Mayor (Number 50)
Alexsandra Annello, First Term District 2 (West Central)
Cassandra Hernández-Brown, First Term District 3 (East)
Sam Morgan, First Term District 4 (Northeast)
Henry Rivera, First Term District 7 (Lower Valley)

Laura D. Prine, Interim City Clerk

Tomás González, City Manager

Courtney Carlisle Niland, District 8, Resignation Letter submitted April 4, 2017, effective April 8, 2017.

Special Runoff Election for District 8 (July 15, 2017)

Cissy Lizárraga, Filling to fill an unexpired term left vacant by Representative Courtney Carlisle Niland. Representative Cissy Lizárraga was sworn in on July 25, 2017. Term began July 25, 2017, and expired 2019.

Cissy Lizárraga, Filling an Unexpired Term, District 8

—SOURCE: *City of El Paso*

Notes

Introduction

1. Floyd Hunter, C. Wright Mills, Robert Dahl, *Who Governs?* Domhoff's edited volume, *Studying the Power Elite*, contains a variety of authors who apply, criticize, and advance the approaches (NY: Routledge 2018). The quote is from his 2014 edition, p. 5.

I. The Fight for Duranguito—
and Against Taxpayer Abuse & Deception

1. Carmen E. Rodríguez, an employment and civil rights attorney with Rodríguez and Associates, has served on various nonprofit boards and is involved with many community organizations.
2. The identity of "the powers that be in El Paso" has evolved over the years as different groups of wealthy and influential individuals have come together to gain political control over public entities and resources. In earlier eras they were the descendants of the old established families. They have been largely male, white, and wealthy and have been the directors of financial institutions, hospitals and other large corporations. They have been developers, industry leaders, and business owners. Their identity is not always precisely known by the public. (See Introduction.)
3. Real Estate Investment Trusts (REIT) are companies that own and most often actively manage income-generating commercial real estate. National Association of Real Estate Investment Trusts, https://www.reit.com/nareit; Aaron Montes, "Margo may have violated ethics rules, disclosure requirement," *El Paso Times*, pp. A1, A6. June 22, 2019.
4. El Paso City Council Minutes, February 15, 2005.
5. El Paso City Council Minutes, September 13, 2005.
6. Open Letter to City Council, *El Paso Times*, June 7, 2006.
7. Glass Beach, a firm with no past and no future, was apparently organized only for this project.
8. Glass Beach Slides Document, Trial Exhibit, Leyva 1. References to trial exhibits hereafter refer to *Ex Parte City of El Paso*, No. D-1-GN-17-001888 (250th Judicial District Travis County, Texas) 2017.

9. The identity of the "powers that be" who directly manipulated the city is not known with certainty. Early on Bill Sanders played an active role, later Woody Hunt participated in lawsuit negotiations in March 2018. Aaron Montes, "Margo may have violated ethics rules, disclosure requirement," *El Paso Times*, pp. A1, A6. June 22, 2019.

10. *Ex Parte City of El Paso*, No. 03-17-00566-CV, 563 S.W.3d 517 (Tex. App.—Austin Nov. 7, 2018, pet. filed). Trial Exhibit Morales 3, Joyce Wilson email dated April 19, 2006.

11. El Paso Downtown Plan 2015 by SMWM. http://www.elpasodowntown-plan.com/Index.aspx?Section=Home&Page=Home and http://www.ci.el-paso.tx.us/_documents/factsheets_downtown/DT%20Plan%20Process,%20May%2006.pdf

12. Christopher Hooks, "Beto Versus the Barrio." *The American Prospect Magazine*, March 15, 2019. https://prospect.org/article/beto-versus-barrio

13. Jordan Construction was the business implicated in bribery charges against County Commissioner Betty Flores in 2006. Several other PDNG members were charged with crimes during a widespread FBI investigation of El Paso County officials and businesses. "Players in the public corruption case," *El Paso Times*, December 11, 2011.

14. https://www.jordanfosterconstruction.com/about-us/history#

15. Alejandro Restrepo and Robert Assael incorporated Rojal Enterprises and used Yellow Balloon and Red Balloon Group to purchase properties in Duranguito. Aaron Montes, "City Buys Properties in Arena Footprint," *El Paso Inc.*, June 12, 2017.

16. http://www.elpasotimes.com/story/news/2017/10/19/city-paying-nearly-triple-assessed-value-downtown-arena-properties-documents-show/780917001/

    https://www.elpasotimes.com/story/news/local/el-paso/2016/10/14/el-paso-downtown-redevelopment-arena-real-estate/92063660//

17. It should be noted that implementation of the plan continued after Mayor Wardy lost his re-lection bid and throughout the John Cook, Oscar Leeser and the current Dee Margo administrations.

18. http://horrowsports.ventures/ and *Ex Parte City of El Paso*, No. 03-17-00566-CV, 563 S.W.3d 517 (Tex. App.—Austin Nov. 7, 2018, pet. filed) Joyce Wilson and David Romo Trial Testimony.

19. *Ex Parte City of El Paso*, No. 03-17-00566-CV, 563 S.W.3d 517 (Tex. App.—Austin Nov. 7, 2018, pet. filed) Goodman Trial Exhibits 1-4 EL Paso Tomorrow PAC Promotional materials.

20. https://borderplexalliance.org/

21. 2012 bond ballot: Museum, cultural, performing arts, and library facilities proposition.

    "SHALL the City Council of the City of El Paso, Texas, be authorized to issue general obligation bonds of the City in the principal amount of $228,250,000 for permanent public improvements and public purposes, to wit: acquiring, constructing, improving, renovating and equipping new and existing library, museum, cultural and performing arts facilities and improvements, including the acquisition of land and rights-of-way for such projects, and acquiring and installing public art related to and being a part of some or all of the foregoing; such projects to include the following: **Museum** Children's Museum; Digital wall at History Museum; Improvements to existing City museum facilities; **Cultural**, Hispanic Cultural Center; **Arts & Entertainment** Multipurpose performing arts and entertainment facility located in Downtown El Paso; [emphasis added] **Library**, Improvements at: Armijo Branch, Clardy Fox Branch...; New Bookmobile, Technology Mobile; Library Materials..." and 2006 Map prepared for PDNG by SMWM, Trial Exhibit Morales 5.

22. *Ex Parte City of El Paso*, No. 03-17-00566-CV, 563 S.W.3d 517 (Tex. App. —Austin Nov. 7, 2018, pet. filed) Goodman Trial Exhibits 1-4.El Paso Tomorrow PAC Promotional materials.
23. Aaron Bracamontes, "Propositions 1 and 2 Quality of Life Bonds approved." *El Paso Times*, November 2012.
24. Historian David Romo had been shown this SMWM map in 2006 by PDNG when he was asked to help identify historic buildings in the barrios. Trial Exhibit Morales 3.
25. "El Paso Historic Landmark Commission suggest the City reconsider the arena location," *The Prospector*, November 8, 2016.
26. Elida S. Perez, "Close-knit Duranguito residents wish to stay," *El Paso Times*, February 25, 2017.
27. Grossman's financial backer remained anonymous for more than a year. In late 2018, J.P. Bryan, noted Texas historic preservationist, chose to engage openly with El Pasoans to promote historic preservation generally and Duranguito specifically. *El Paso Times*, December 17, 2018.
28. *Ex Parte City of El Paso*, No. 03-17-00566-CV, 563 S.W.3d 517 (Tex. App. —Austin Nov. 7, 2018, pet. filed) City's proposed Findings of Fact and Conclusions of Law.
29. *Ex Parte City of El Paso*, No. 03-17-00566-CV, 563 S.W.3d 517 (Tex. App. —Austin Nov. 7, 2018, pet. filed) Morales respondents' proposed Findings of Fact and Conclusions of Law.
30. *Ex Parte City of El Paso*, No. 03-17-00566-CV, 563 S.W.3d 517 (Tex. App. —Austin Nov. 7, 2018, pet. filed).
31. *Max Grossman v. City of El Paso*. No. 2017-DCV-2528 (384th Judicial Dist. Ct. El Paso Co. Tex).
32. TEX.NAT.RES.CODE §191.0525.
33. The city and landlords lost no time in vacating the apartments by offer-

ing the resident/tenants relocation stipends. http://diario.mx/El_Paso/
2017-05-01_53af0ad0/denuncian-expulsion-de-residentes-de-duranguito/
34. *El Paso Times*, December 17, 2018; *El Paso Herald Post*, January 29, 2019.

II. The Baseball Park Boondoggle

1. Professor Emeritus Oscar J. Martínez, with a PhD in history and author of books about the binational region, taught at UTEP, moved to the University of Arizona as a Regents' Professor, and returned home to El Paso after retirement.
2. *El Paso Inc.*, November 4, 2012.
3. "Plan El Paso," p. 3.19.
4. "New PAC to promote quality of life bond," *El Paso Inc.*, July 29, 2012; "Downtown arena support tainted?" *El Paso Inc.*, September 16, 2012.
5. *El Paso Inc.*, July 8, 2012.
6. *El Paso Inc.*, July 9, 2012.
7. Larry Francis, "City Hall Armageddon," *El Paso Inc.*, August 12, 2012.
8. https://www.scribd.com/document/109368433/Salazar-El-Paso-Lawsuit
9. Nestor Valencia, "Time for City Council to Reconsider," *El Paso Inc.*, August 16, 2012.
10. *El Paso Inc.*, August 26, 2012.
11. Anonymous interview with a then city council member conducted by author, June 14, 2019.
12. Kevin J. Delaney and Rick Eckstein, *Public Dollars, Private Stadiums: The Battle Over Building Sports Stadiums* (Rutgers University Press, 2003), pp. 183–184.
13. https://kfoxtv.com/news/local/city-of-el-paso-says-ballpark-debt-sched-uled-to-be-paid-by-2021.
14. Email from Dr. Max Grossman to author, May 25, 2018. Grossman's calculations based on city of El Paso data.
15. "Welfare for Team Owners," *The Week*, November 2, 2018, p. 11.

III. Political Contributions:
The Best Candidates Money can Buy?

1. Professor Emerita Kathleen (Kathy) Staudt, with a PhD in political science, taught for forty years at UTEP and wrote books about international development, political economy, and the border, culminating in her latest, *Border Politics in a Global Era* (2017).
2. White and Anglo are used interchangeably in this piece and book.
3. https://www.elpasotexas.gov/municipal-clerk/city-elections/campaign-finance-reports.

4. The first city manager was Joyce Wilson. She was succeeded by Tommy González. They are appointed by the city council.

5. Incumbent Joe Wardy obtained sizeable sums, with the infamous Bob Jones donating the largest amount ($3,000). Jones later was convicted of embezzlement in 2011 for the way he categorized "disabled" workers (monolingual Spanish speakers) in his nonprofit business.

6. See picture and powers outlined: https://www.elpasotexas.gov/mayor/powers-and-duties-of-the-mayor.

7. https://www.huntcompanies.com/what-we-do/military-communities

8. See Hunt Family Foundation: http://www.huntfamilyfoundation.com/.

9. At the national level, the Supreme Court's Citizens United decision of 2010 was a setback to those troubled by the influence of big money in political decisions and the lack of transparency of donors and their beneficiaries.

10. Manuel Gutiérrez and Kathleen Staudt, "Governing our Borderlands Commons," in *Binational Cooperation at the US-Mexico Border*, Tony Payan, ed. (Tucson: University of Arizona Press, forthcoming), provides figures from the latest local/*municipio* elections. The recent exception occurred in 2018, given the enthusiasm for El Paso candidate Beto O'Rourke running to replace Ted Cruz, U.S. Senator from Texas. In 2018, local elections moved from the more typical low-voter turnout in spring (first Saturday) to the first Tuesday in November when other candidates stand for office.

11. "Texas Civic Health Index," University of Texas at Austin Annette Strauss Institute (2018): https://moody.utexas.edu/centers/strauss/texas-civic-health-index.

IV. El Paso's Public Debt Obligations v. "Quality of Life"

1. Rosemary Neill's professional experience includes service in state, regional and local governments as well as large and small not-for-profit organizations. She has served on numerous nonprofit boards of directors. Professor Emerita Kathleen (Kathy) Staudt, with a PhD in political science, taught for forty years at UTEP and wrote books about international economy, and the border, culminating in her latest, *Border Politics in a Global Era* (2017).

2. The Borderplex Alliance (see Section I), whose mission is to attract business to the binational region, lists incentives such as property tax abatements for up to ten years from governments at the local, state, and school district levels, with two staff people available for new businesses to call: https://borderplexalliance.org/site-selection/incentives/el-paso-and-texas. Cary Westin, formerly Director of Economic Development

for the city of El Paso and now the Deputy City Manager for Economic Development, was Vice President for Business Development for Defense and Clean Tech at the Borderplex Alliance from 2011–2014. Most of the business leaders in Borderplex Alliance were once affiliated with the Paso del Norte Group before it disbanded.

3. $2,225,681,585 (2018 Comprehensive Annual Financial Report).

4. These strategies were rolled out at a large event at El Paso Community College on April 18, 2019, and in a webinar on May 8, 2019, conducted by the El Paso Collaborative for Academic Excellence, in both of which Staudt participated. For the websites of the organizations mentioned in this paragraph, see https://www.borderplexjobs.com www.creeed.org and https://www.utep.edu/epcae/

5. https://www.elpasotimes.com/story/news/2019/05/02/city-official-contemplates-library-and-pool-closures-meet-budget-restraints/3642261002/

6. https://www.elpasotimes.com/story/entertainment/2019/04/11/new-water-park-lazy-river-built-central- el-paso/3435653002/

7. https://www.elpasotexas.gov/~/media/files/coep/office%20of%20management%20and%20budget/fy19 %20budget/fy%202019%20adopted%20budget%20book%20online%20version%20-%20optimized- new.ashx?la=en

8. The city sponsored "focus groups," for which the city's communication personnel prepared and sent a descriptive email to participants. The "results" all seemed to reinforce the city strategies, reminiscent of the manipulation reported in Section II. Those of us in CFC who "chimed in" with substantive comments did not see them in this report, undifferentiated by region of the city and/or "alternative" opinions.

V. The Controversial Selection of Dr. Heather Wilson as UTEP President

1. Dr. Oscar J. Martínez is a retired professor who taught at various universities, but primarily at UTEP and the University of Arizona. He is the author of many books and other publications on Mexico, Mexican Americans, and the U.S.-Mexico borderlands. Currently he serves as the head of the El Paso Social Justice Education Project and the co-coordinator of the Community First Coalition, a confederation of grass-roots groups in El Paso.

2. https://www.forbes.com/sites/charlestiefer/2015/08/31/lockheed-fined-4-7-million-for-fraudulent-taxpayer-paid-lobbying-with-most-corrupt-ex-rep-wilson/?fbclid=IwAR3kJ4zjD45K6AZNt65J-McvJqmoZib56aefe-G3IpOSga_H7jzN4JFm4C0I#6a0f586b46c0.

3. Ibid.; https://www.citizensforethics.org/press-release/crew-releases-third-annual-most-corrupt-members-of-congress-report/; https://www.politico.com/story/2017/02/records-show-how-air-force-nominee-skirted-lobbying -restrictions-234780.

4. https://www.elpasotimes.com/story/opinion/2019/04/12/uteps-next-president-not-representative-el-paso-jose-rodriguez/3449548002/

5. https://www.change.org/p/texas-board-of-regents-utep-deserves-better-stop-anti-lgbtq-heather-wilson-from-becoming-utep-s-next-president.

6. "Charles Koch gave $25m to our university. Has it become a rightwing mouthpiece?" *The Guardian*, May 2, 2019;
      https://www.facingsouth.org/2015/02/meet-the-southern-tycoons-helping-fund-the-koch-br.html; https://www.denverpost.com/2014/02/10/column-taking-a-touchy-look-at-links-to-politically-active-billionares/.

VI. The Cheap, Disrespectful, and Contemptuous City Plan to Squeeze a Cultural Center into the Historic Downtown Library

1. Dr. Oscar J. Martínez is a retired professor who taught at various universities, but primarily at UTEP and the University of Arizona. He is the author of many books and other publications on Mexico, Mexican Americans, and the U.S.-Mexico borderlands. Currently he serves as the head of the El Paso Social Justice Education Project and as co-coordinator of the Community First Coalition, a confederation of grass-roots groups in El Paso.

VII. The Ongoing Saga of the "Lost Dog Trail"

1. This essay is based on a report prepared by Marilyn Guida, with contributions from Marshall Carter-Tripp, PhD; Judy Ackerman; Sharon Miles-Bonart, PhD; Rick Bonart, DVM; Janaé Reneaud Field; Richard Teschner, PhD. The collective is grateful for Guida's extensive knowledge of land issues in El Paso and for making her report available to us. For a meticulous version of her longer report, with all the here-to-fore dated meeting minutes, numbered agenda items, and websites cited, contact Marilyn Guida c/o the CFC (communityfirst915@gmail.com). For more insight on smarter growth, see Charles Marohn, "The more we grow, the poorer we become," August 22, 2018, https://www.strongtowns.org/journal/2018/8/22/the-more-we-grow-the-poorer-we-become (reprinted from *Public Management*).

2. The name Lost Dog emerged after a trail user lost his dog.

3. El Paso Water, Land Study for Westside PSB Properties, June 2005. City of El Paso Planning Department, Transmountain Corridor and Northwest Regulating Plan 2013, January 15, 2013.

4. PSB Minutes, February 14, 2018, Item 12.

5. https://www.elpasotimes.com/story/news/local/el-paso/2018/08/07/city-council-denies-petition-reserve-land-northwest-el-paso-lost-dog-trail-open-space/924356002/.

6. Based on comments made by Dr. Rick Bonart, leader of the Lost Dog effort, in an interview with reporter Aaron Montes, "El Pasoans vote overwhelmingly to preserve Lost Dog, open space on the west side," *El Paso Times*, May 4, 2019. On validation in this (and the following) paragraph, El Paso City Clerk letter to Dr. Rick Bonart, September 12, 2018.

7. Ibid., in Montes.

8. Details in this paragraph come from https://www.elpasotimes.com/story/news/local/el-paso/2018/08/07/city-council-denies-petition-reserve-land-northwest-el-paso-lost-dog-trail-open-space/924356002, and https://www.kvia.com/news/el-paso/el-pasoans-overwhelmingly-approve-preservation-of-open-space-in-northwest/1075266170.

9. *El Paso Inc.*, November 4, 2018.

Conclusion

1. Oscar J. Martínez, *The Chicanos of El Paso: An Assessment of Progress* (El Paso: Texas Western Press, Southwestern Studies, 1980).

COMMUNITY FIRST COALITION

Founded in January 2019. CFC, P.O. Box 12681, El Paso, Texas, 79913. communityfirstcoalition.org; facebook.com/cfc915/; Contact: communityfirst915@gmail.com

Mission

To bring about improvements in social, economic, and political conditions in El Paso through collaborative planning, policy advocacy, and community action.

Vision

CFC aspires to bring our diverse border community closer together to make El Paso a better city for all its residents. Our members promote the respectful and humanitarian treatment of the most vulnerable, building close and trusting relationships with communities on both sides of the border, and sharing resources and opportunities with those in need. CFC defines "community" as a network of human and environmental relationships ranging from one extended family to whole neighborhoods, schools, churches and community organizations. El Paso is a complex web of multiple communities that intersect and are interdependent. There is wisdom, beauty and strength in these networks, and we consider them our priority. Our communities face challenges, but we know that they, too, have creative solutions to any issues facing them. We believe that people in these communities have a right to information, to transparency and accountability in government, and to effective civil engagement.

Constituent Organizations

American Library Association—El Paso Chapter; Border Network for Human Rights; Border Regional Library Association; Chicano History Project; El Chuqueño; Hope Border Institute; Lincoln Center; LULAC Council 132; Main Library Friends; Mexican American Cultural Institute; Paso del Sur; Raza Organize; Reforma Library Organization; Social Justice Education Project; Texas Library Association—El Paso Chapter; Sancturary4LongevityProject; Union for Development and Quality of Life; UTEP Retired Professors; Velo Paso Bicycle-Pedestrian Coalition; Wise Latina International.

CPSIA information can be obtained
at www.ICGtesting.com
Printed in the USA
FSHW020949060220
66875FS